trotman

Aston University

Careers Centre Resource Library

Please return this book by the last stamped date
All late returns will be charged at 50p per day

1 2 DEC 2011

Getting into Dental School
This fifth edition published in 2007 by Trotman and Company Ltd
2 The Green, Richmond, Surrey TW9 1PL

© Trotman and Company Limited 2007

Editorial and Publishing Team
Author James Burnett
Editorial Mina Patria, Editorial Director; Jo Jacomb, Editorial Manager;
Catherine Travers, Managing Editor; Ian Turner, Production Editor
Production Ken Ruskin, Head of Manufacturing and Logistics;
James Rudge, Production Artworker
Sales and Marketing Sarah Lidster, Marketing Manager
Advertising Sarah Talbot, Advertising Manager

British Library Cataloguing in Publication Data
A catalogue record for this book is available from the British Library.

ISBN 978 1 84455 115 6

Typeset by Ian Turner.
Printed and bound in Great Britain by Creative Print and Design (Wales).

CONTENTS

ACKNOWLEDGEMENTS

This book would not have been possible without the help of many people. In particular, I would like to thank Dr Anne Aiken, Dr Stephen Fenny, Dr Neva Patel, Saba Saied, Maya Waterstone, the dental students who helped to paint a picture of life at dental school, the admissions tutors from the dental schools who gave us the information on admissions, and the British Dental Association for providing much of the factual material on careers in dentistry. However, I would like to emphasise that although the information in the book has been provided by experts, most of the views expressed are my own, and any mistakes are down to me.

James Burnett
November 2006

For up-to-date information on dental schools,
go to www.mpw.co.uk/getintomed

INTRODUCTION

'Why would you want to spend all day looking into people's mouths? I can't think of anything worse!' This, typically, is the reaction when you tell someone that you want to become a dentist. The fact that you are reading this book probably means that you have realised that dentistry offers far more than this. What, then, are the attractions of a career in dentistry?

If you talk to dentists, they mention some or all of the following as being reasons why they chose dentistry:

- An interest in human biology and dental issues
- The opportunity to have day-to-day contact with a wide range of people
- Freedom to choose your own patients, and to be your own boss
- Flexibility in choosing the length of the working day
- Working as part of a team
- Working with your hands, and being able to do so creatively
- Status and respect.

The number of women choosing to become dentists is increasing because it is possible, once qualified, to work part time, and to combine family life with a career (which, of course, applies to men as well!).

There are, of course, some negative aspects of dentistry that need to be considered. In its highly informative advice sheet on careers in dentistry, the British Dental Association urges prospective dentists to consider a number of aspects including stress, lack of job and financial security (because of self-employment), lack of career progression and, last but by no means least, the boredom that can accompany repetitive routine tasks. If you are worried about any of these, you should talk to your own dentist to see how he/she feels about them. Some dentists will warn students against going into the profession without being aware that dentistry suits people who are prepared to work hard, and who enjoy being with other people.

Dentistry is not just about teeth, but about oral health in general. The reason why a dental course lasts five years is that the teaching covers physiology, biomedical sciences, pharmacology, the effects of anaesthetics and other components common to both medicine and dentistry. Dentists are often the first to spot medical problems that might otherwise go unnoticed until the problem has worsened. An example of this is oral cancer. There are over 3000 new cases of oral cancer each year, and about half this number die from the disease. This figure is comparable with more highly publicised cancers, such as skin cancer.

In 2005, there were 2621 applicants for dentistry, according to UCAS. Of these, 1187 gained places (2.2 applicants per place). After a fall in the number of applicants in recent years, it is increasing again. Of the 2005 applicants, the ratio of women to men was about 52:48, and the ratio of places gained was about 56:44. In other words, women were on average slightly more successful than men in their applications.

In order to increase access to dental treatment, in 2006 the government announced a new dental school at the Peninsula Medical School (which will offer four-year courses for science graduates and healthcare professionals) with 100 new dental training places shared between Peninsula, Liverpool University and Leeds University. The new Peninsula Dental School will take its first intake in 2007. King's also runs a four-year graduate entry programme aimed at biomedical or health-related graduates.

So what does the recent rise in applicants for dentistry mean? Almost certainly, that grade requirements for entry into dental school will continue to rise, in order to differentiate between all the applicants. In the late 1990s, when application numbers were lower, candidates often received BBC offers, whereas now the standard offer is likely to be AAB or even AAA.

Probably even more so than medicine, candidates must be able to demonstrate not only academic ability and the right personal qualities, but also commitment. Dentistry is such a specialised career that requires a combination of many skills, that applicants who cannot demonstrate these rarely get offers.

What are the skills and personal qualities that a dentist requires? The main ones are:

- An enjoyment of science
- The ability to be reassuring, particularly to those who are scared or in pain
- Enjoyment of being around other people
- Manual dexterity
- Self-motivation
- A caring and sympathetic nature
- Stamina
- The ability to work as part of a team.

Some of these will not surprise you. It would be hard to be a successful dentist if you could not bear to be around other people, and unsympathetic dentists end up with few patients. If you do not enjoy science, you would be unlikely to gain the necessary grades at A level, or to pass the dental school examinations.

If you believe that you have these qualities, the next step is to investigate what being a dentist is actually like, by organising work experience or work shadowing. This is a vital part of your application – it is unlikely that you will be considered unless you have done so – but more importantly, it is a chance for you to see whether it is the right career for you. Whatever the attractions, if you cannot see yourself enjoying the job for the next forty years, choose another career.

Many people are unaware that dentists are usually self-employed, and the amount of money they earn is directly related to how many patients they see. Without stamina, and the self-motivation to work hard without someone keeping an eye on you, you are unlikely, at least at the start of your career, to earn as much as you might hope. A survey by the British Dental Association (2003) revealed that the average student debt on graduating was about £15,000 (22 per cent up on the previous year) and, once qualified, a dentist needs not only to earn enough to support him or herself, but also to begin paying off the debt.

Before looking at the applications and admissions processes in more detail, you may be interested to read what a dental student and a recently qualified dentist have to say about their choice of career.

CASE STUDY

Saba Saied is a fourth year dental student at Barts and the London, Queen Mary's School of Medicine and Dentistry. 'I came to London to study dentistry, having studied the International Baccalaureate at an international school in Austria. I always had an interest in the sciences and knew that my career would involve them, as well as involving people and the chance to use my hands. Before starting the course, I took a year out to travel and to gain work experience, both of which helped me to gain a sense of the real world. I also learnt a great deal about myself.

'Throughout the course, I have tried to maintain a balance between work and a social life. The first two years were pre-clinical, and were spent at the

Mile End campus, a friendly place full of atmosphere and students from a wide range of courses. Here we were taught the theoretical basics of medical science. The time between lectures gave us the chance for self-directed learning, and the tutorials gave us the chance to improve our understanding of the material covered in the lectures and the practicals.

'The next three years are spent at Whitechapel, where the medics and dentists are based. The dental school is buzzing all of the time, with patients of all shapes, sizes and colours. We have a great deal of responsibility, including booking our patients, calling them up and arranging appointments. I really enjoy the chance to put communication skills, psychology and sociology into practice.

'The first contact with our patients was exciting and nerve-racking. We had been well prepared and had been given the opportunity to watch and assist the students in the years above us, but now the onus was on us. You get to realise that experience is the only way to learn about clinical dentistry and dealing with patients.

'The social life is great. There is always something happening, from quiz nights to the college's clubs and societies, and although having only one year left makes me glad that I will soon be going out into the world to start working, I will miss student life enormously.

'Since starting here, I have found that dentistry is more than just a career that involves work: it is basically about patients.'

CASE STUDY   Dr Neva Patel qualified from King's six years ago. 'When I qualified, I wasn't sure whether I wanted to become a GDP (General Dental Practitioner), or to work in another field, such as orthodontics or paedodontics. I decided to spend a year in the hospital to gain experience of a range of dental fields. Working as a House Officer was a very comfortable way of being introduced to dentistry – I saw four to five patients a session, and was able to call upon experts if and when the need arose. However, I did not particularly enjoy hospital politics, and I also realised that I did not want a career in research, and so I started my Vocational Training [VT], the compulsory year's training under a dentist in a dental practice.

'I was very lucky with my trainer who was extremely helpful and supportive, and I enjoyed the year at the practice so much that I stayed on to practise there, and have been there ever since. Amongst my group of friends who qualified as dentists, I was the only one to stay on at the same practice after VT. I started off gently, seeing perhaps five to ten patients a day, so that I could spend time on the treatment. At first, I could take up to an hour on a filling, but I soon became quicker and more confident. The big difference between now and when I first started is that I am not worried about what will come in through the door – I feel that I can cope with anything. The job does have stressful times, of course, particularly when dealing with difficult or aggressive patients. However much you are taught about stress management and dealing with anxious patients at dental school, it cannot prepare you for the real thing.

'Some patients can be aggressive because they are scared. I find that the best way to deal with nervous patients is to explain to them exactly what I am doing at all times. Whenever I use a new instrument, I tell the patient what it is for, and what I will do with it. I explain why I am taking X-rays, and the likely lifetime of the treatment that I am performing. Otherwise, they cannot see what is going on, and can become more frightened.

'The best part of the job, for me, is when my patients are genuinely pleased with the treatment: I find it very gratifying when new patients are referred by existing ones. I also like the flexibility of the job, and the fact that I can control my hours.

'My position is slightly unusual because I am a salaried dentist. This enables me to spend more time with my patients if they need it, and to devote some time to teaching patients about dental health. I don't have to worry about filling my day to maximise my earnings. It means that there is a limit to what I earn, but it also adds to job satisfaction.'

CASE STUDY Stephen Fenny has been a practice owner working in London for 15 years. 'What I get out of being a dentist is the people that I treat, not the mechanics of the job. The job is repetitive and often stressful, particularly as I run my own business and have to be aware of the balance between providing the best possible treatment for my patients and the economics of running the practice. Today, I saw 29 patients – slightly more than usual because of school half-term – and I need to ensure that I juggle my time effectively, so that an unexpected problem with one patient does not cause delays for others. Being reassuring and comforting throughout the day, whilst trying to deal with a large number of patients, brings about its own form of stress. Having said that, for me, people are the excitement of the job, and the thing that makes being a dentist enjoyable and worthwhile.'

CASE STUDY Martin Jones is a first year dental student studying in London. Martin started studying Dentistry in London in October. He sat A levels at a school in Birmingham, and had wanted to be a dentist since his final year of GCSEs. Martin had originally thought about Pharmacy – his father is a hospital pharmacist and his mother is a nurse at another hospital – but a friend of his family who was a dentist invited him to spend a week shadowing him in his practice. Martin found the experience fascinating: 'Some of my friends had done work experience in hospitals with doctors, and they didn't really enjoy themselves. There was lots of hanging around and they were not allowed to do anything that involved patients. My time with the dentist was different. He showed me everything that was happening and let me help the nurse make fillings and take impressions. I was surprised that all of the patients agreed to let me watch what was happening. I suppose that they trusted the dentist and were happy to do what he asked.'

Martin chose Biology, Chemistry, Physics and Ceramics as his AS levels. 'To be honest, I wasn't desperately keen on Ceramics or Physics – I would have preferred English and French. However, my careers teacher thought that Ceramics might help to demonstrate manipulative skills, and the dentist that I shadowed said that Physics had helped him during his course.' He dropped Ceramics after AS with a C grade, and went on to achieve ABB in the science subjects. Martin got two interviews, one at Birmingham and the other at King's. Both concentrated heavily on his work experience. 'My advice to anyone considering Dentistry is to get as much work experience as possible, and to ask questions whenever possible. Find out about everything the dentist does, and write it down at the end of the day. Funnily enough, none of the interviewers asked me about manual dexterity, so I needn't have done Ceramics – although I actually enjoyed it in the end.'

Martin's first few months studying Dentistry have been hard work. 'I haven't really had a chance to relax yet – there is an enormous workload, and the social life is very hectic. I am coping because I know it is what I want to do. A couple of others on the course are having doubts because they originally wanted to do Medicine.'

**ABOUT THIS
BOOK**

This book is divided into five main sections:
- Getting an interview
- Getting an offer
- Results day
- Dental school and beyond
- Current issues.

Chapter 1 deals with the preparation that you need to undertake in order to make your application as irresistible as possible. It includes advice on work experience, how to choose a dental school and the UCAS application procedure, and finishes with a checklist for you to tick off the important steps in making your application. Chapter 2 provides advice about what to expect at interview, and how to ensure that you come across as a potential dentist. Chapter 3 describes the steps that you need to take if you are holding an offer, or if you do not have an offer but want to gain a place through Clearing. Chapters 4 and 5 provide background information on dentistry and on dental issues.

On page 48 there is advice and information for 'non-standard' applicants – mature students, graduates, students who have studied arts A levels and retake students.

Like another book in this series, *Getting into Medical School*, this book is designed to be a route map for potential dentists, rather than a guide to dentistry as a profession. The British Dental Association, or your own dentist, should be the starting points for more detailed information on what being a dentist entails.

For the latest news on dentistry and dental schools go to www.mpw.co.uk/getintomed

Although entrance requirements have been given in terms of A level grades throughout the book, information for students who have studied Scottish Highers, the IB and other examinations is given on page 17.

1

GETTING AN INTERVIEW

In order to gain a place at dental school, you have to submit a UCAS application. Before you do this, however, you need to be sure that you have investigated dentistry as thoroughly as you can. Most people have (or think that they have) a good idea about medicine as a career because it gets such a wide variety of publicity. Almost every night, there is a medical programme on television – *Casualty*, *Holby City*, *ER*, *Grey's Anatomy* and *Green Wing*, to name but a few – but there is considerably less exposure to dentistry. How many films can you name that feature dentists? Most people can only get as far as Laurence Olivier in *Marathon Man* – not an ideal role model! On TV, Kyle MacLachlan in *Desperate Housewives* and Robert Lindsay in *My Family* also portray very flawed characters.

It is also fair to say that dentistry is a narrower profession than medicine, and it is vital that you are aware of what being a dentist entails on a day-to-day basis before committing yourself. This is not to say that all dentists do the same thing. As we shall see later, dentistry offers a variety of career paths, but there are fewer options available to dentists than to doctors.

When your UCAS application is received by the dental school, it will not be on its own but in a batch, possibly of many. The selectors will have to consider it, along with the rest, in between the demands of other aspects of their jobs. If your application is badly worded, uninteresting or lacking the things that the selector feels are important, it will be put on the 'reject without interview' pile. A typical dental school might receive 800 applications, which have to be reduced to 300 to be called for interview. You can only be called for interview on the basis of your UCAS application. The selectors will not know about the things that you have forgotten to say and they can only get an impression of you from what is in the application. I have come across too many good students who never got an interview, simply because they did not think properly about their UCAS application: they relied on their hope that the selectors would somehow see through the words and get an instinctive feeling about them.

The following sections will tell you more about what the selectors are looking for, and how you can avoid common mistakes. Before looking at how the selectors go about deciding who to call to interview, there are a number of important things that you need to think about.

WORK EXPERIENCE

Most admissions tutors would agree that the absolute minimum amount of time that prospective dental students should spend work-shadowing dentists is two weeks – anything less than this will be unlikely to allow you to appreciate the realities of dentistry as a career. Ideally, you should aim to spend three or four weeks with one or more dentists, or to help out in a dental surgery on a regular basis over several months.

The first thing to do is to arrange your work experience. If you are lucky, your school will have a scheme running where they arrange this for you. This saves you the hard work of contacting dental practices, but the disadvantage of this is that you will be unable to impress the selectors with your dynamism and determination because you will not be able to say 'I arranged my work experience myself.' If your school does not operate such a scheme, you have two options: to use any contacts that your family or friends have; or to approach local dentists. To do this, get the names and addresses of local dental practices from the telephone directory or the British Dental Association (www.bda.org). You should write a formal letter, and include the name of a referee, someone who can vouch for your interest in dentistry as well as your reliability. Your careers teacher, housemaster/mistress or form teacher would be ideal. An example of a suitable letter is given below.

I Melchester Road
Melchester MC2 3EF
0123 456 7890

Mr P Mackie [Telephone the practice for the name of one of the dentists.]
Pain-free Dental Clinic
123 High Street
Melchester MCI IAB

I October 2006

Dear Mr Mackie

I am in the first year of my A level studies, and I am interested in a career in dentistry. In order to find out more about dentistry, I would like to shadow a dentist, preferably for a week. I would be extremely grateful if you would be prepared to meet me, in order to discuss whether it would be possible for me to spend some time at the Pain-free Dental Clinic.

If you require a reference, please contact my careers teacher. His contact details are:

Mr N Townson, Head of Careers
Melchester High School
Melchester MCI 2CD

I look forward to hearing from you.

Yours sincerely

L M Johnson

Lucy Johnson (Miss)

Shadowing dentists is useful for three reasons:

1 | It will help you to decide whether you really want to be a dentist.
2 | It will demonstrate your seriousness to admissions tutors.
3 | You may, if you can demonstrate to the dentist that you are serious about dentistry, be able to ask him/her for a reference.

THINGS TO LOOK OUT FOR DURING WORK EXPERIENCE

THE VARIETY OF TREATMENTS AVAILABLE TO PATIENTS

Make sure that you know what you are observing. Ask the dentist or nurse for the technical names of the procedures that you see, and for information on the materials and equipment used. Ask about the advantages and disadvantages of different types of filling, implants or dentures. Make sure that you are aware not only of how damaged teeth are repaired, but also about preventative dentistry, orthodontics and oral hygiene. You should also try to discuss the dentist's role in identifying other problems, such as mouth cancer.

WORKING AS A DENTIST

Ask the dentist about his/her life. Find out about the hours, the way in which dentists are paid, the demands of the job, and the career options open to dentists. Find out what the dentists like about the job, and what they dislike.

TIPS FOR WORK EXPERIENCE

- Dress as the dentists dress: be clean, tidy and reasonably formal.
- Ask intelligent questions about the procedures that you witness, and keep a diary of the things that you see.
- Offer to help the dentist or the receptionists with routine tasks.
- Show an interest in all that is going on around you.

CHOICE OF SCHOOL

Once you have completed your work experience, and are sure that you want to be a dentist, you need to research your choice of dental school. There are various factors that you should take into account:

- The type of course
- The academic requirements (see pages 16 and 71)
- Location
- Whether the dental school is part of a large university, or a stand-alone medical and dental school.

The next step is to get hold of the prospectuses. If your school does not have spare copies, telephone the dental schools and they will send you copies free of charge. Most dental schools have very informative websites that carry extra information on admissions policies. Once you have narrowed down the number of dental schools to, say, six or seven, you should try to visit them in order to get a better idea of what studying there will be like. Your school careers department will have details of open days (or you could telephone the dental schools directly), and some will arrange for you to be shown around at other times of the year as well. Don't simply select your dental schools because someone tells you that they have good reputations or that they are easier to get into, because you will be spending the next five years of your life at one of them, and if you do not like the place, you are unlikely to last the course.

Apart from talking to current or ex-dental students or careers advisers, there are a number of other sources of information to help you to choose. The *Guardian* publishes its own league table of dental schools, ranked by a total score that combines a number of assessment categories, including teaching scores, student–staff ratios and job prospects. The 2005 table placed King's first, followed by Leeds, Queen Mary, Sheffield and Dundee. Of course, there is no such thing as a bad dental school in the UK, and league tables only tell you a small part of the whole story. League tables are no substitute for visiting the dental schools, looking at the course content in detail, and reading the prospectuses. However, if you are interested in the league tables, they can be found at http://education.guardian.co.uk/universityguide2006.

ACADEMIC
REQUIRE-
MENTS

In addition to the grades required at A level, all of the dental schools specify the minimum grades that they require at GCSE. This varies from dental school to dental school, but it is unlikely that you will be considered unless you have at least five A or A* grades, with at least B grades at science, English and Mathematics. If your grades fall below these requirements, you need to get your referee to comment on them, either to explain why you underperformed (illness, family disruption etc) or why they expect your A level performance to be better than your GCSE grades indicate.

If you are worried about achieving the right grades, you should think carefully about choosing at least two dental schools that accept retake candidates. The table on page 71 shows you which dental schools consider students who have not achieved the minimum grades at the first attempt. The reason for putting two (or more) of these dental schools is that many places will give preference to students who applied there first time round. Some even specify it as a requirement for retakers.

In addition to specifying A level grades, some dental schools will ask for a minimum grade in the free-standing AS level. As important is the fact that AS levels contribute 50% to the total A level score, and poor AS level grades will make it difficult, if not impossible, to achieve A grades at A level. AS level grades also give admissions tutors more to go on than GCSE grades and A level predictions alone, since the AS grades will be published in the August preceding your UCAS application and will feature on it. For the student, this means that the first year of A levels is as important as the second.

The typical entry grade requirements of the dental schools are shown on page 71. You should also check the schools' prospectuses for details of GCSE requirements and AS level requirements. Some dental schools, for example, specify that they require one of the AS subjects to be an art or humanity, rather than all being sciences or mathematics.

OTHER QUALIFICATIONS

If you are not studying A levels, you should check with each dental school about their requirements. Listed below is a rough indication of what they might ask for:

Scottish Highers: AAAAA–AABBB at Advanced Higher/Higher level. Higher level Chemistry and Biology are required, with at least one at Advanced Higher level.

International Baccalaureate: 6,6,5 and 35–36 points overall. Chemistry plus one other science or mathematical subject to be taken at Higher level with passes in English and Mathematics at Standard level.

European Baccalaureate: 80% overall, with 80% in each science option; Chemistry and another science as full options.

NON-DENTAL CHOICES

There are six spaces on the UCAS application, but only four of these can be used to select dentistry courses. The remaining spaces can either be left blank, or can be filled with other choices. Whatever you do, do not put down medicine or veterinary science as your fifth and sixth choices, because not only will the medical school or veterinary school reject you, but it will be obvious to the selectors that you are not committed to dentistry. You are allowed to choose courses such as dental hygiene or therapy, but this is also not a good idea since students who take alternative dental courses tend to get frustrated and drop out. If you decide that you would be happy to accept an alternative to dentistry if you are unsuccessful, by all means choose another course as long as you feel able to justify the choice at interview. However, my advice is to leave it blank because:

- It demonstrates to the selectors that you are committed to becoming a dentist.
- You do not run the risk of feeling obliged to accept a place on a course that you do not wish to take. If you are unsuccessful in your application to your chosen four dental schools, you might be able to gain a place through Clearing, as long as you have not accepted something else.

UKCAT

Some dental schools now require applicants to sit the UKCAT (United Kingdom Clinical Aptitude Test) before they apply. The dental schools currently using the test are Cardiff, Dundee, Glasgow, King's, Manchester, Newcastle, Queen Mary and Sheffield. Registration for the 2007 test (for applicants applying for 2008 entry) starts in the first week of June 2007. You register online (www.ukcat.ac.uk) and sit the test at an external test centre. The current cost is £60 if you the test in the EU and £95 elsewhere. The 2006 test, which lasted 90 minutes, comprised four sections:

- Verbal reasoning
- Quantitative reasoning
- Abstract reasoning
- Decision analysis.

From 2007, there is likely to be an extra section involving written, rather than multiple choice, responses. Although the UKCAT website tries to discourage students from doing any preparation for the test other than sitting the practice test available on the website, students who sat it in 2006 found that the more practice they had on timed IQ-type tests, the better prepared they felt. In the reference section of most bookshops, there are a number of books that contain practice questions of a similar type to the UKCAT. Some useful titles are listed on the website that accompanies this book (www.mpw.co.uk/getintomed).

PERSONAL STATEMENT

The personal statement is your chance to show the selectors that:

- You have thought about why you want to be a dentist
- You have investigated the profession
- You are the right sort of person for their dental school.

Almost all applicants now submit their applications via Apply on www.ucas.com; follow the instructions and use the drop-down menus and help features to avoid errors. This system can be completed at any computer linked to the internet and forwarded to your referee very easily. See *How to Complete Your UCAS Application* for details.

The personal statement is your opportunity to demonstrate to the selectors that you have not only researched dentistry thoroughly, but also have the right personal qualities to succeed as a dentist. Do not be tempted to write the statement in the sort of formal English that you find in, for example, job applications. Read through a draft of your statement, and ask yourself the question *'Does it sound like me?'* If not, rewrite it. Avoid phrases such as *'I was fortunate enough to be able to shadow a dentist ...'* when you really just mean *'I shadowed a dentist ...'* or *'I arranged to shadow a dentist ...'* A sample statement can be found below.

Why Dentistry?

My interest in dentistry started when my local dentist came to my school to give a careers talk. Up until that point, my view of dentistry was based on my own nervousness when I visited the dentist. However, the talk showed me that there was more to dentistry than simply filling cavities. I began to realise that dentistry involved an understanding of science, an ability to keep up to date with new technologies, and a chance to run a business, as well as allowing me to use my communication skills.

Work Experience

I spent two weeks shadowing my local dentist. During this time, the dental nurse was away for a day, so I was able to help the dentist with simple tasks such as sterilising instruments. I was also able to help the receptionist with filing and talking to patients in the waiting room. This showed me the need for sensitivity and confidentiality. I was also able to discuss what dentistry as a career involves. I enjoyed my time at the Pain-free Dental Clinic, and so I arranged to get a Saturday job at another local dental practice, helping the nurse. I have been doing this for nine months. The dentist let me practise using the drill on some extracted teeth, and I realised that it was much more difficult than it looked. I was very interested in finding out about what the dentist thought about the new NHS reforms and whether they were likely to improve working conditions for dentists and the availability of treatment for patients.

Activities and Responsibilities

I am head of my form at school, which involves working with the teachers to ensure that everything runs smoothly. I play football for the 1st XI, and cricket for the 2nd XI. I play the clarinet in the school orchestra, and for relaxation I am learning to play the guitar. As well as my Saturday job, I go to my local old people's home once a week to talk to the residents. As part of the school charity committee, I have helped to organise a sponsored fast, which raised £986 for Shelter. I enjoy going out with my friends at the weekend, and am planning to travel around Europe with three others during the summer.

WHY DENTISTRY?

A high proportion of UCAS applications contain a phrase like *'From an early age I have wanted to be a dentist because it is the only career that combines my love of science with the chance to work with people.'* Admissions tutors not only get bored with reading this, but it is also clearly untrue: if you think about it, there are many careers that combine science and people, including teaching, pharmacy, physiotherapy and nursing. However, the basic ideas behind this sentence may well apply to you. If so, you need to personalise it. You could mention an incident that first got you interested in dentistry – a visit to your own dentist, a conversation with a family friend, or a lecture at school, for instance. You could write about your interest in human biology, or a biology project that you undertook when you were younger to illustrate your interest in science, and you could give examples of how you like to work with others. The important thing is to back up your initial interest in dentistry with your efforts to investigate the career.

WHAT HAVE YOU DONE TO INVESTIGATE DENTISTRY?

This is where you describe your work experience. It is important to demonstrate that you gained something from the work experience, and that it has given you an insight into the profession. You should give an indication of the length of time that you spent at each dental practice, what treatments you observed, and your impressions of dentistry. You could comment on what aspects of dentistry attract you, what you found interesting or on something that surprised you.

Here is an example of a description of a student's work experience that would not impress the selectors:

> *I spent three days at my local dental practice. I saw some patients having fillings, and a man whose false teeth didn't fit. It was very interesting.*

The example below would be much more convincing because it is clear that the student is interested in what was happening.

During my two weeks at the Pain-free Dental Clinic, I was able to shadow two dentists and a hygienist. I watched a range of treatments including fillings, a root canal, extractions and orthodontic treatment. I found particularly interesting the fact that, although both dentists had very different personalities, they both related well to the patients, who seemed to find them very reassuring. A number of things surprised me, in particular, how demanding a dentist's day is.

With luck, the selectors may pick on this at interview, and ask questions about the methods that the dentists used to relax their patients, or the demands of dentistry.

PERSONAL QUALITIES

As a dentist, you will be working with others throughout your career. To qualify as a dentist, you will study alongside maybe fifty others in your year, for five years. The person reading your UCAS application has to decide two things: whether you have the right personal qualities to become a successful dentist, and whether you will cope with and contribute to dental school life. To be a successful dentist, you need to be able to relate to other people; to survive and enjoy dental school, you need to be able to get on with a wide range of people, too. Unlike school life, where many of the activities are organised and arranged by the teachers, almost all of the social activities at university are instigated and organised by the students. For this reason, the selectors are looking for people who have the enthusiasm and ability to motivate others, and to be prepared to give up their own time to arrange sporting, dramatic, musical or social activities.

How, then, does the person reading your personal statement know whether you have the qualities that they are looking for? They will expect to read about some of the following:

- Participation in team events
- Involvement in school plays or concerts
- Positions of responsibility
- Work in the local community

■ Part-time or holiday jobs
■ Charity work.

The selectors will be aware that some schools offer more in the way of activities and responsibilities than others, and they will make allowances for this. You don't have to have been on a school expedition to India, or to be head girl to be considered, but you need to be able to demonstrate that you have taken the best possible advantage of what is on offer. The selectors will be aware of the type of school or college that you have come from (there is a section of the UCAS application that your referee fills in) and consequently, the opportunities that are open to you. What they are looking for is that you have grasped these opportunities.

THE REFERENCE

As well as your GCSE results and your personal statement, the selectors will take your reference into account. This is where your head, housemaster or head of sixth form writes about what an outstanding person you are, how you are the life and soul of the school, how you are on target for three A grades at A level and why you will become an outstanding dentist. For him or her to say this, of course, it has to be true. The referee is expected to be as honest as possible, and to try to accurately assess your character and potential. You may believe that you have all of the qualities, academic and personal, necessary in a dentist, but unless you have demonstrated these to your teachers, they will be unable to support your application. Ideally, your efforts to impress them will have begun at the start of the sixth form (or before): you will have become involved in school activities, you will have been working hard at your studies and you will be popular with students and teachers alike. However, it is never too late, and some people mature later than others so if this does not sound like you, start to make efforts to impress the people who will contribute to your reference.

As part of the reference, your referee will need to predict the grades that you are likely to achieve. As you will see from the table on page 71, the minimum requirement is AAB. If you are predicted lower than this, it is unlikely that you will be considered. Talk to your teachers and find out whether you are on target for these grades. If not, you need to either a) work harder or more effectively – and make sure that your teachers notice that you are doing so, b) get some extra help either at school or outside, for instance an Easter revision course or c) delay submitting your UCAS application until you have your A level results. If you decide on this option, make sure that you use your gap year wisely (see below).

WHEN TO SUBMIT THE UCAS APPLICATION

The closing date for receipt of the application by UCAS is 15 October. Late applications are accepted by UCAS, but the dental schools are not obliged to consider them, and because of the pressure on places, it is unlikely that late applications will be considered. Although you can submit your application any time between the beginning of September and the October deadline (remembering to get it to your referee at least two weeks before the deadline so that he/she has time to prepare the reference), most admissions tutors admit that the earlier the application is submitted, the better your chance of being called for interview. Your best bet is to talk to the person who will deal with the form in the summer term of your first year of A levels, and work on your personal statement and choice of dental school over the summer holidays so that it is ready to submit at the start of the September term.

DEFERRED ENTRY

Most admissions tutors are happy to consider students who take a gap year, and many encourage it. However, if you are considering this, you need to make sure that you are going to use the time constructively. A year spent watching daytime TV is not going to impress anybody, whereas independent travelling, charity or voluntary work either at home or abroad, work experience or a responsible job will all indicate that you have used the time to develop independence and maturity. Above all, make sure that whatever you do with the year involves regular contact with other people.

You can either apply for deferred entry when you submit your UCAS application, in which case you need to outline your plans in your personal statement, or apply in

September following the publication of your A level results. If you expect to be predicted the right grades, and the feedback from your school or college is that you will be given a good reference, you should apply for deferred entry, but if you are advised by your referee that you are unlikely to be considered, you should give yourself more time to work on your referees by waiting until you have your A level results.

WHAT HAPPENS NEXT?

About a week after UCAS receives your application, they will send you a Welcome Letter listing all of your choices. Check this carefully – make sure that the universities and courses are correct (a common mistake is to select the foundation year – the 'pre-dental' year – rather than the start of the course proper), and that your name and address are also correct. Remember also to inform UCAS if you change address.

The next correspondence you will receive, if you are lucky, is likely to be from the dental schools, asking you to attend an interview. You can also keep track of offers or rejections by using the online facility on the UCAS website. You will be given a password by UCAS to access this. Do not be alarmed if you do not hear anything soon after UCAS has sent you your Welcome Letter. Some dental schools interview on a first come, first served basis whilst others wait until all applications are in before deciding who to interview. It is not uncommon for students to hear nothing until after Christmas.

If you are unlucky, you will receive notification from UCAS telling you that you have been rejected by one or more of the dental schools. Don't despair: you may hear better news from another of the schools that you applied to. Even if you get four rejections, the worst thing that you can do is to give up and decide that it is no longer worth working hard. On the contrary, if this does happen, you should become even more determined to gain high grades so that you can apply either through Clearing, or the following year. The process of making Clearing applications is discussed in Chapter 3.

CHECKLIST

- ☐ Two weeks' work-shadowing?
- ☐ Right GCSEs?
- ☐ On target for AAB?
- ☐ Looked at all dental schools' prospectuses?
- ☐ Been to open days?
- ☐ Registered for the UKCAT?
- ☐ Maximum four choices on UCAS application?
- ☐ Personal statement demonstrates commitment, research, personal qualities, communication skills and manual dexterity?

2

GETTING AN OFFER

If the selectors like the picture that the UCAS application has painted of you, they will call you for interview. The purpose of the interview is to allow them to see whether this picture is an accurate one, and to investigate whether you have a genuine interest in dentistry.

The interviewers will generally ask you questions of the following types:

- Those designed to relax you so that they can assess your communication skills
- Those designed to investigate your interest and suitability for dentistry
- Those designed to get a clearer picture of your personal qualities.

QUESTIONS TO GET YOU RELAXED

Question: *How was your journey here today?*
Comment: The interviewers are not really interested in the details of your journey. Do not be tempted to give them a minute-by-minute account of your bus journey ('*... and then we waited for six minutes at the road works on Corporation Street ...*'), or to simply say '*OK*'. Say something like '*It was fine, thank you. The train journey took about two hours, which gave me the chance to catch up on some*

reading.' With a bit of luck, they will ask you what you read, which gives you the chance to talk about a book, newspaper article or an item in *New Scientist*.

Question: *Tell me why you decided to apply to Melchester.*
Comment: Another variation on this might be *'How did you narrow your choice down to four dental schools?'* The panel will be looking for evidence of research, and that your reasons are based on informed judgement. Probably the best possible answer would start with *'I came to your open day ...'* because you can then proceed to tell them why you like their university so much, what impressed you about the course and facilities and how the atmosphere of the place would particularly suit you. Even if you are unable to attend open days, try to arrange a formal or informal visit before you are interviewed so that you can show that you are aware of the environment, both academic and physical, and that you like the place. If you know people who are at the dental school or university, so much the better. You should also know about the course structure: the prospectus will give detailed information. Given the choice between a candidate who is not only going to make a good dentist, but clearly wants to come to their institution, and another who may have the right qualities but does not seem to care whether it is there, or somewhere else that he/she studies, who do you think the selectors will choose?

Answers to avoid are ones such as *'Reputation'*, unless you know in detail the areas for which the dental school is highly regarded, *'It's in London, and I don't want to move away from my friends'*, *'You take a lot of retake students'* or *'My dad says it is easy to get a place here.'*

WARNING: Do your homework by reading the prospectus and looking at the website. Although on the surface all dental courses appear to cover broadly the same subjects, there are big differences between the way courses are delivered, and in the opportunities for patient contact, and your interviewers will expect you to know about their course.

A good answer could be *'I came to an open day last summer, which is why I have applied here. I enjoyed the day, and was impressed by the facilities, and by the comments of the students who showed us around because they seemed so enthusiastic about the course. Also, my cousin studied English at the university and I visited her, and got to sample the atmosphere of the town.'* There are variations on this question. The interviewers may ask you what you know about the course, or about the dental school. In all cases, this is your chance to show the interviewers that you are desperate to come to their dental school.

QUESTIONS ABOUT DENTISTRY

Question: *Why do you want to be a dentist?*
Comment: The question that all interviewees expect. Given that the interviewers will be aware that you are expecting the question, they will also expect your answer to be carefully planned. If you look surprised, and say something like *'Um ... well ... I haven't really thought about why ...'* you can expect to be rejected. Other answers to avoid are ones along the lines of *'The money'*, *'I couldn't get into medicine'*, *'I want to help people'* or *'I like inflicting pain'*.

Many students are worried that they will sound insincere when they answer this question. The way to avoid this is to try to bring in reasons that are personal to you, for instance, an incident that started your interest (perhaps a visit to your own dentist), or an aspect of your work experience that particularly fascinated you. The important thing is to try to express clearly what interested you, rather than generalise your answers. Rather than saying *'dentistry combines science, working with people and the chance to have control over your career'* – which says little about you – tell the interviewers about the way that your interest progressed. Here is an example of a good answer:

Although it seemed strange to my friends, I used to enjoy going to the dentist when I was young. This was because my dentist explained things very clearly and patiently, and I was interested in what was happening around me. When I was thinking about my career, I arranged to shadow another dentist, and the more time I spent at the surgery, the more I realised that this would really suit me. This also gave me the chance to find out about what being a dentist is really like. The things about dentistry that I particularly enjoy are ...

> **WARNING:** Do not learn the above passage and repeat it at your interview. Ensure that your answer is not only personal to you, but also honest.

With luck, the interviewers will pick up on something that you said about work experience, and ask you more questions about this.

Since *'Why do you want to be a dentist?'* is such an obvious question, interviewers often try to find out the information in different ways. Expect questions such as *'When did your interest in dentistry start?'*, or *'What was it about your work experience that finally convinced you that dentistry was for you?'*

Question: *I see that you spent two weeks with your dentist. Was there anything that surprised you?*
Comment: Variations on this question could include *'Was there anything that particularly interested you?'*, *'Was there anything you found off-putting?'* or simply *'Tell me about your work experience'*. What these questions really mean is *'Are you able to show us that you were interested in what was happening during your work experience?'* Returning to the original question, answering either *'Yes'* or *'No'* without explanation will not gain you many marks. Similarly, saying *'Yes, I was surprised by the number of patients who seemed very scared'* says nothing about your awareness of the dentist's approach to his/her patients. However, answering *'Yes, I was surprised by the number of patients who seemed very scared. What struck me, however, was the way in which the dentist dealt with each patient as an individual, sometimes being sympathetic, sometimes explaining things in great detail and sometimes using humour to relax them. For instance ...'* shows that you were interested enough to be aware of more than the most obvious things. Sentences that start with *'For example ...'* and *'For instance ...'* are particularly important as they allow you to demonstrate your interest. In order to be able to give examples, you should keep a diary of things that you saw during your work experience so that you do not forget. You should revise from this before your interview, as if you were revising for an examination.

Question: *I see that you try to keep up to date with developments in dentistry. Can you tell me about something that you have read about recently?*

Comment: If you are interested in making dentistry your career, the selectors will expect you to be interested enough in the subject to want to read about it. Good sources of information are *New Scientist*, the British Dental Association website and the national newspapers. You should get into the habit of looking at a broadsheet newspaper every day to see if there are any dentistry-related stories. Note that the question uses the word recently: recent does not mean an article you read two years ago – keep up to date. You could, for instance, say *'There was a recent article in* New Scientist, *about the different types of bacteria present in the mouth, only a few of which are responsible for tooth decay. At present, anti-bacterial toothpastes and mouthwashes kill all bacteria, including ones that play a beneficial role. Scientists are now working on antibacterials that only target specific, harmful bacteria.'*

Question: *During your work experience, you had the chance to discuss dentistry with the practitioner. What do you know about the way NHS dentists are paid?*

Comment: You must be aware of the nuts and bolts of running a dental practice. You should be aware that, whilst NHS GPs are paid according to a capitation scheme (by the number of patients on their books), NHS dental practitioners are paid for the treatment that they perform. You should also have an idea about what a dentist earns and what proportion of it goes back into running the practice. Similar questions might focus on how much dentists are paid for different types of treatment, or how much NHS patients pay for treatment.

Question: *What qualities should a dentist possess?*

Comment: These have been discussed on page 3 and page 21. However, don't simply list them. The question has not been asked because the interviewer is puzzled about what these qualities are; it has been asked to give you a chance to show that a) you are aware of them, and b) you possess them. The best way to answer this is to use phrases such as *'During my work experience at the Pain-free Dental Clinic, I was able to observe/talk to the dentist, and I* became aware that …', or 'Communication is very important. For instance, when I was shadowing my dentist, there was a patient who …'. Try always to relate these general questions to your own experiences.

Question: *What is the difference between tooth erosion and tooth decay?*
Comment: The interviewer is clearly not asking this question because he/she does not know the answer. The reason for the question is to find out whether you have learned about common dental problems through your discussions with dentists during work experience. As a prospective dentist, you will be expected to use technical terms more accurately than your friends who do not want to be dentists. A good answer might be: *'I asked this question to my own dentist last time I went to see her. She explained that tooth erosion is the wearing away of the tooth enamel, which can be caused by things like fizzy drinks (which are acidic) or by grinding your teeth while you are asleep. Decay is caused by the reaction between sugar and the bacteria in plaque.'*

Question: *Dentistry requires a high degree of manual dexterity. Do you possess this?*
Comment: Manual dexterity means being able to perform intricate tasks with your hands. Dentists have to work in a confined and sensitive area (the mouth) using precision instruments in situations where accuracy is vital and where there is little margin for error. If you have trouble picking up a coffee cup without knocking it over, or if you always press the wrong keys when you work on a computer, dentistry may not be the best career for you. The interviewers will need reassurance that you have the manipulation skills to be able to work on other people's teeth. Good examples of tasks that require a high degree of manual dexterity include sewing, embroidery, model-making, touch-typing and playing a musical instrument. If you are not able to give an example of your own manipulative skills, take up a hobby that involves precision work now, before it is too late. Some admissions tutors like interviewees to bring in examples of their handiwork. A particularly good example of this is a student who brought in a denture that she had made during her work experience. This allowed her not only to demonstrate that

she possessed the necessary skills, but also to talk about the role of the dental technician within a practice.

> **WARNING:** Do not lie about the example of manual dexterity that you describe. One admissions tutor tells the story of a boy who claimed that he liked icing cakes in his spare time. He brought in photographs of some of the cakes he had iced, but it became clear, after very little questioning, that it was his mother who had actually done the work. This did not go down well with the panel, as you can imagine!

QUESTIONS TO FIND OUT WHAT SORT OF PERSON YOU ARE

Question: *What do you do to relax?*
Comment: Don't say *'Watch TV'* or *'Go to the pub'*. Mention something that involves working or communicating with others, for instance sport or music. Use the question to demonstrate that you possess the qualities required in a dentist. However, don't make your answer so insincere that the interviewers realise that you are trying to impress them. Saying *'I relax most effectively when I go to the local dental surgery to shadow the dentist'* will not convince them.

Question: *How do you cope with stress?*
Comment: Dentistry can be a stressful occupation. Dentists have to deal with difficult people, those who are scared and those who react badly when in a dental surgery. Furthermore, there are few 'standard' situations: everyone's mouth and teeth are different, as are their problems, and things can go wrong. In these circumstances, the dentist cannot panic, but must remain calm and rational. In addition, the nature of the profession means that dentists must always be aware of the financial aspects of running a business. The interviewers will want to make a judgement as to whether you will be able to cope with the demands of the job.

Having been through it themselves, it is unlikely that they will regard school examinations as being particularly stressful. Hard work, yes, but not as stressful as training to be a dentist or practising as a dentist. What they are looking for are answers that demonstrate your calmness and composure when dealing with others. You could relate it to your work experience, or your Saturday job. Dealing with a queue of angry and impatient customers demanding to know why their cheeseburgers are not ready can be difficult. Other areas that can provide evidence of stress-management are school expeditions, public speaking, or positions of responsibility at school or outside.

HOW TO SUCCEED IN THE INTERVIEW

Question: *I see that you enjoy reading. What is the most recent book that you have read?*

Comment: The question might be about the cinema or theatre, but the point of it is the same: to get you talking about something that interests you. Although it may sound obvious, if you have written that you enjoy reading on your UCAS application, make sure that you have actually read something recently. Admissions tutors will be able to tell you stories about interviewees who look at them with absolute surprise when they are asked about books, despite it featuring in the personal statement. Answers such as *'Well … I haven't had much time recently, but … let me see … I read* Elle *last month, and … oh yes … I had to read* Jane Eyre *for my English GCSE'* will do your chances no good at all. By all means put down that you like reading, but make sure that you have read an interesting novel in the period leading up to the interview, and be prepared to discuss it.

You should prepare for an interview as if you are preparing for an examination. This involves revision of your work experience diary so that you can recount details of your time with a dentist, revision of the newspaper, website and *New Scientist* articles that you have saved and revision of all the things that you have mentioned on your personal statement. When you are preparing for your A levels you sit a mock examination so that the real thing does not come as a total surprise; when you are preparing for an interview, have a mock interview so that you can get some feedback on your answers. Your school may be able to help you. If not, independent sixth-form colleges usually provide a mock interview service. Friends of your parents may also be able to help. There is a list of practice interview questions below.

MOCK INTERVIEW QUESTIONS

1 | Why do you want to be a dentist?
2 | What have you done to investigate dentistry?
3 | Why does dentistry interest you more than medicine?
4 | What are the ideal qualities that a dentist should possess?
5 | Do you possess these qualities?
6 | Give me an example of how you cope with stress.
7 | Why did you apply to this dental school?
8 | Did you come to our open day?
9 | During your work experience, did anything surprise you?
10 | During your work experience, did anything shock you?
11 | Is your own dentist good at communicating with his patients?
12 | Tell me about preventative dentistry.
13 | What is orthodontics?
14 | Why do dentists recommend the fluoridation of water supplies?
15 | What are the arguments against fluoridation of water supplies?
16 | What are amalgam fillings made of?
17 | What are white fillings made of?
18 | There has been a good deal of negative publicity about mercury fillings. Do you think that they are dangerous?
19 | If you had to organise a campaign to improve dental health, how would you go about it?
20 | What is gingivitis?
21 | How are NHS dentists funded? Is it the same for GPs?
22 | Should dental treatment be free on the NHS?
23 | How much does an average dentist earn?
24 | Have you read any articles about dentistry recently?
25 | What advances can we expect in dental technology/treatment in the future?
26 | What have you done to demonstrate your commitment to the community?
27 | What would you contribute to this dental school?
28 | What are your best/worst qualities?
29 | What was the last novel that you read? Did you like it?

30 | What was the last play/film that you saw? Did you like it?

31 | What do you do to relax?

32 | What is your favourite A level subject?

33 | What grades do you expect to gain in your A levels?

34 | Do dentists treat children differently from adults?

35 | What precautions need to be taken with patients who are HIV positive?

36 | What is an overbite?

37 | What do you know about forensic dentistry?

38 | What is the role of the dental nurse/technician?

39 | How does teamwork apply to the role of a dentist?

40 | Did the dentists you talked to enjoy their jobs?

41 | What is the difference between tooth erosion and tooth decay?

42 | What role does a dentist have in diagnosing other medical problems?

43 | What do you know about the new NHS reforms for dentistry?

44 | What do you know about the new government contract for dentists?

45 | What are the reasons for the increasing use of composite fillings?

46 | Can you think why dentists might be concerned about the increasing use of composite fillings?

Appearance and body language are important. The impression that you create can be very influential. Remember that if the interviewers cannot picture you as a dentist in future years, they are unlikely to offer you a place.

BODY LANGUAGE

- Maintain eye contact with the interviewers.
- Direct most of what you are saying to the person who asked you the question, but occasionally look around at the others on the panel.
- Sit up straight, but adopt a position that you feel comfortable in.
- Don't wave your hands around too much, but don't keep them gripped together to stop them moving. Fold them across your lap, or rest them on the arms of the chair.

SPEECH

- Talk slowly and clearly.
- Don't use slang.
- Avoid saying 'Erm ...', 'You know', 'Sort of'.
- Say hello at the start of the interview, and thank the interviewer(s) and say goodbye at the end.

DRESS AND APPEARANCE

- Wear clothes that show that you have made an effort for the interview. You do not have to wear a business suit, but a jacket and tie (men), or a skirt and blouse (women) are appropriate.
- Make sure that you are clean and tidy.
- If appropriate, shave before the interview (but avoid overpowering aftershave).
- Clean your nails and shoes.
- Wash your hair.
- Avoid (visible) piercings, earrings (men), jeans and trainers.

If possible, video your mock interview so that you are aware of the way that you come across in an interview situation.

AT THE END OF THE INTERVIEW

You may be given the opportunity to ask a question at the end. Bear in mind that the interviews are carefully timed, and that your attempts to impress the panel with 'clever' questions may do quite the opposite. The golden rule is: only ask a question if you are genuinely interested in the answer (and which, of course, you were unable to find during your careful reading of the prospectus).

QUESTIONS TO AVOID

- *What is the structure of the first year of the course?*
- *Will I be able to live in a hall of residence?*
- *When will I first have contact with patients?*

As well as being boring questions, the answers to these will be available in the prospectus. You have obviously not done any serious research.

QUESTIONS YOU COULD ASK

■ *I haven't studied Biology at A2 level. Do you think I should go through some Biology textbooks before the start of the course?*

This shows that you are keen, and that you want to make sure that you can cope with the course. It will give them a chance to talk about the extra course they offer for non-biologists.

■ *Do you think I should try to get more work experience before the start of the course?*

Again, an indication of your keenness.

■ *Earlier, I couldn't answer the question you asked me on fluoridation of water supplies. What is the answer?'*

Something that you genuinely might want to know.

■ *How soon will you let me know if I have been successful or not?'*

Something you really want to know.

Remember: if in doubt, don't ask a question. End by saying *'All of my questions have been answered by the prospectus and the students who showed me around the dental school. Thank you very much for an interesting day.'* Smile, shake hands (if appropriate) and say goodbye.

STRUCTURING THE INTERVIEW

The selectors will have a set of questions that they may ask, designed to assess your suitability and commitment. If you answer *'Yes'* or *'No'* to most questions, or reply only in monosyllables, they will fire more and more questions at you. If, however, your answers are interesting and also contain statements that interest them, they are more likely to pick up on these, and you are, effectively, directing the interview. If you are asked questions that you have prepared for, there will be less time for the interviewers to ask you questions that might be more difficult to answer. For instance, at the end of your answer to a question about work experience, you might say:

... and the dentist was able to explain the effect of new technology on dentistry ...'

The interviewer may then say:

I see. Can you tell me about how technology is changing dentistry?

You can then embark on an answer about new types of polymers used in fillings, for instance. At the end of your explanation, you could finish with:

... which will reduce the need for amalgam fillings that contain mercury, which some people believe have an adverse effect on a person's health.

You may then be asked about the possible problems with mercury, and so on.

Of course, this does not always work, but you would be very unlucky not to have at least one of these 'signposts' that you placed in front of them followed.

HOW YOU ARE SELECTED

During the interview, the panel will be assessing you in various categories. Whether or not the interview appears to be structured, the interviewers will be following careful guidelines so that they can compare candidates from different interview sessions. Some panels adopt a conversational style, whereas others are more formal. The scoring system will vary from place to place, but in general, you will be assessed in the following categories:

- Reasons for the choice of dental school
- Academic ability
- Motivation for dentistry
- Awareness of dental issues
- Personal qualities
- Communication skills.

You are likely to be scored in each category, and the dental school will have a minimum mark that you will have to gain if you are to be made an offer. If you are below this score, but close to it, you may be put on an official or unofficial waiting list. If this happens, you may be considered in August, should there be places available.

If you are offered a place, you will receive a letter from the dental school telling you what you need to achieve in your A levels. This is called a conditional offer. Post-A level students who have achieved the necessary grades will be given unconditional offers. If you are unlucky, all you will get is notification from UCAS saying that you have been rejected. If this happens, it is not necessarily the end of the road that leads you to a career in dentistry. You may be successful in Clearing, or as a post-A level applicant. The way to go about this is described on page 42.

When UCAS has received replies from all of your choices, they will send you a statement of offers. You will then have about a month to make up your mind about where you want to go. If you only have one offer, you have little choice but to accept it. If you have more than one, you have to accept one as your firm choice, and may accept another (a lower offer) as your insurance choice. If the place where you really want to study makes a lower offer than one of your other choices, do not be tempted to choose the lower offer as your insurance, since you are obliged to go to the dental school that you have put as your firm choice if you achieve the grades. Even if you narrowly miss, you may still be accepted by your first choice. If you decide that you do not want to go there, once the results are issued, you will have to withdraw from the UCAS system for that year.

If you are unsuccessful, there remains the option of studying dentistry overseas (see page 50).

3

RESULTS DAY

The A level results will arrive at your school on the third Thursday in August. The dental schools will have received them a few days earlier. You must make sure that you are not away on the day the results are published. Don't wait for the school to post the results slip to you. Get your teachers to tell you the news as soon as possible. If you need to act to secure a place, you may have to do so quickly.

The dental school admissions departments are well organised and efficient, but they are staffed by human beings. If there were extenuating circumstances that could have affected your exam performance and which were brought to their notice in June, it is a good idea to ask them to review the relevant letters shortly before the exam results are published.

If you received a conditional offer and your grades equal or exceed that offer, congratulations! You can relax and wait for your chosen dental school to send you joining instructions. One word of warning: you cannot assume that grades of AAC satisfy an ABB, or even BBB, offer.

The paragraphs that follow take you through the steps you should follow if you need to use the Clearing system because you have good grades but no offer. They also explain what to do if your grades are disappointing.

WHAT TO DO IF YOU HOLD NO OFFER

These days very few applicants get into dental school through Clearing. Table 2 (page 72) shows that very few schools keep places open and, of those that do, most will choose to allow applicants who hold a conditional offer to slip a grade rather than dust off a reserve list of those they interviewed but didn't make an offer to. Still less are they likely to consider applicants who appear out of the blue – however high their grades. That said, it is likely that every summer one or two dental schools will have enough unfilled places to consider a Clearing-style application.

If you hold three A grades but were rejected when you applied through UCAS you need to let the dental schools know that you are out there. The best way to do this is by fax or by email. Fax and phone numbers are listed in the *UCAS Handbook*. If you live nearby, you can always deliver a letter in person, talk to the office staff and hope that your application will stand out from the rest.

Set out opposite is a sample letter/fax. Don't copy it word for word!

Do not forget that your referee may be able to help you. Try to persuade him or her to ring the admissions officers on your behalf – he or she will find it easier to get through than you will. If your head teacher is unable/unwilling to ring, then he or she should, at least, send a fax or email in support of your application. It is best if both faxes/emails arrive at the dental school at the same time.

If you are applying to a dental school that did not receive your UCAS application, ask your head to fax or send a copy of the form. In general, it is best to persuade the dental school to invite you to arrange for the UCAS application to be sent.

If, despite your most strenuous efforts, you are unsuccessful, you need to consider applying again (see below). The other alternative is to use the Clearing system to obtain a place on a degree course related to dentistry and hope to be accepted on the dental course after you graduate. This option is described on page 49.

WHAT TO DO IF YOU HOLD AN OFFER BUT MISS THE GRADES
If you have only narrowly missed the required grades (this includes the AAC grade case described above), it is important that you and your referee fax/email the dental school to put your case before you are rejected. Another sample letter follows overleaf.

---

1 Melchester Road
Melchester MC2 3EF
0123 456 7890

16 August 2007

Miss M D Whyte
Admissions Officer
Melchester University School of Dentistry
University Road
Melchester MC1 4GH

Dear Miss Whyte

UCAS No 08-123456-7

I have just received my A level results, which were:
Biology A, Chemistry A, English A
I also have an A grade in AS Art

You may remember that I applied to Melchester but was rejected after interview/was rejected without an interview. I am still very keen to study dentistry at Melchester and hope that you will consider me for any places which may now be available.

My head teacher supports my application and is faxing you a reference. Should you wish to contact him, his details are: Mr C Harrow, Tel: 0123 456 7891, Fax: 0123 456 7892.

I can be contacted at the above address and could attend an interview at short notice.

Yours sincerely

L M Johnson

Lucy Johnson (Miss)

I Melchester Road
Melchester MC2 3EF
0123 456 7890

16 August 2007

Miss M D Whyte
Admissions Officer
Melchester University School of Dentistry
University Road
Melchester MC1 4GH

Dear Miss Whyte

UCAS No 08-123456-7

I have just received my A level results, which were:
Chemistry A, Biology A, English C

I hold a conditional offer from Melchester of ABB and I realise that my grades may not meet that offer. Nevertheless I am still determined to study dentistry and I hope you will be able to find a place for me this year.

May I remind you that at the time of the exams I was recovering from glandular fever. A medical certificate was sent to you in June by my head teacher.

My head teacher supports my application and is faxing you a reference. Should you wish to contact him, his details are: Mr C Harrow, Tel: 0123 456 7891, Fax: 0123 456 7892.

I can be contacted at the above address and could attend an interview at short notice.

Yours sincerely

L M Johnson

Lucy Johnson (Miss)

If this is unsuccessful, you need to consider retaking your A levels and applying again (see below). The other alternative is to use the Clearing system to obtain a place on a degree course related to medicine and dentistry and hope to apply to the dental course after you graduate. This option is described on page 49.

RETAKING YOUR A LEVEL(S)

The grade requirements for retake candidates are normally higher than for first timers (usually AAB or even AAA). You should retake any subject where your first result was below B and you should aim for an A grade in any subject you do retake. It is often necessary to retake a B grade. Take advice from the college that is preparing you for the retake.

Most subjects allow you to retake some or all units in January. In some cases, you might be close enough to the grade boundary to risk retaking just one unit, but bear in mind that the more units that you retake, the fewer extra marks you have to achieve on each in order to reach the magical figure of 480 UMS – the A grade boundary. It is also worth remembering that A2 units are harder than AS units, and so you are more likely to be able to gain the extra marks that you need by retaking an AS unit or two than by relying on the A2 units alone.

If you simply need to improve one subject by one or two grades and can retake the exam on the same syllabus in January, then the short retake course (September to January) is the logical option. If, on the other hand, your grades were DDE and you need to retake all three subjects, then you probably need to spend another year on your retakes. You would find it almost impossible to cope with three subjects and achieve an increase of nine or ten grades within the 17 weeks or so that are available for teaching between September and January.

Independent sixth-form colleges provide specialist advice and teaching for students considering A level retakes. Interviews to discuss this are free and carry no obligation to enrol on a course, so it is worth taking the time to talk to their staff before you embark on A level retakes.

REAPPLYING TO DENTAL SCHOOL

Many dental schools discourage retake candidates (see Table 1, page 71) so the whole business of applying again needs careful thought, hard work and a bit of luck.

The choice of dental schools is narrower than it was the first time round. Don't apply to the dental schools that discourage retakers unless there really are special, extenuating circumstances to explain your disappointing grades. The following are examples of excuses which would not be regarded by admissions tutors as extenuating circumstances.

> I went skiing at Easter, and was unable to revise properly because it was too cold in the evenings for me to work.

> I left my bag on the bus the week before the exams, and all of my notes were in it, so I couldn't do any revision.

> We moved house a month before the exams, and a removal man trod on my notes, and I couldn't revise properly from them.

Some reasons are acceptable to even the most fanatical opponents of retake candidates:

- Your own illness
- The death or serious illness of a very close relative.

These are just guidelines and the only safe method of finding out if a dental school will accept you is to write and ask them. A typical letter is set out opposite. Don't follow it word for word and do take the time to write to several dental schools before you make your final choice.

The format of your letter should be:

- Opening paragraph
- Your exam results – set out clearly and with no omissions
- Any extenuating circumstances – a brief statement
- Your retake plan – including the timescale
- A request for help and advice
- Closing paragraph.

Make sure that your letter is brief, clear and well presented. You can type or word-process it, if you wish, but you should write 'Dear Sir/Madam' and 'Yours faithfully' by hand. If you have had any previous contact with the admissions staff you will be able to write 'Dear Dr Smith' and 'Yours sincerely'. Even if you go to this trouble the pressure on dental schools in the autumn is such that you may receive no more than a photocopied standard reply to the effect that, if you apply, your application will be considered.

Apart from the care needed in making the choice of dental school, the rest of the application procedure is as described in the first part of this guide.

---

1 Melchester Road
Melchester MC2 3EF
0123 456 7890
16 August 2007

Miss M D Whyte
Admissions Officer
Melchester University School of Dentistry
University Road
Melchester MC1 4GH

Dear Miss Whyte

Last Year's UCAS No 08-123456-7

I am writing to ask your advice because I am about to complete my UCAS application and would very much like to apply to Melchester.

You may remember that I applied to you last year and received an offer of AAB/was rejected after interview/was rejected without an interview.

I have just received my A level results, which were:
Biology B, Chemistry D, English E
I also have a B grade in AS Art

I plan to retake Chemistry in January after a 17-week course and English over a year. If necessary, I will retake Biology from January to June. I am confident that I can push these subjects up to AAA grades overall.

What worries me is that I have heard that some dental schools do not consider retake candidates. I am very keen not to waste a slot on my UCAS application (or your time) by applying to schools that will reject me purely because I am retaking.

I am very keen to come to Melchester, and would be extremely grateful for any advice that you can give me.

Yours sincerely

L M Johnson

Lucy Johnson (Miss)

NON-STANDARD APPLICATIONS

So far, this book has been concerned with the 'standard' applicant: the UK resident who is studying at least two science subjects at A level and who is applying from school or who is retaking immediately after disappointing A levels. Dental schools accept a small number of applicants who do not have this 'standard' background. The main non-standard categories are covered below.

THOSE WHO HAVE NOT STUDIED SCIENCE A LEVELS

If you decide that you would like to study dentistry after having already started on a combination of A levels that does not fit the subject requirements for entry to dental school, you can apply for the 'pre-dental course'. This is offered at five university faculties of dentistry: Bristol, Cardiff, Dundee, King's and Manchester. The course covers elements of chemistry, biology and physics and lasts one academic year.

If your pre-dental application is rejected, you will have to spend a further two years taking science A levels at a sixth-form college. Independent sixth-form colleges offer one-year A level courses and certain subjects can be covered from scratch in a single year. However, only very able students can cover A level Chemistry and Biology in a single year with good results. You should discuss your particular circumstances with the staff of a number of colleges in order to select the course that will prepare you to achieve the A level subjects you need at the grades you require.

OVERSEAS STUDENTS

The competition for the few places available to overseas students is fierce and you would be wise to discuss your application informally with the dental school before submitting your UCAS application. Many dental schools give preference to students who do not have adequate provision for training in their own countries. You should contact the dental schools individually for advice.

Information about qualifications can be obtained from British Council offices or British Embassies.

Overseas students are liable for the full cost of tuition. For dentistry, the fees vary, depending on the stage of the course, from about £11,000 for the pre-clinical parts of the course, to a minimum of about £21,000 for clinical teaching.

MATURE STUDENTS AND GRADUATES

Each year a small percentage of the entrants to dentistry are graduates, usually aged between 22 and 30 (see Table 2, page 72). In exceptional circumstances, candidates who are over 30 may be considered. In general, there are two types of mature applicants:

- Those who have always wanted to study dentistry but who failed to get into dental school when they applied from school in the normal way
- Those who came to the idea later on in life, often having embarked on a totally different career.

The first type of mature applicant has usually followed a degree course in a subject related to medicine or dentistry, obtained a good grade (minimum 2.1) and hopes to gain some exemption from part of the pre-clinical course. These students have an uphill path into dentistry because their early failure tends to prejudice the selectors. Nevertheless, they do not have the problem of taking science A levels at a late stage in their education.

If you want to follow this option you should apply through Clearing for one of the dentistry-related degrees, such as:

- Anatomy
- Biomedical Sciences
- Biochemistry
- Human Biology
- Medical Science
- Pharmacology
- Physiology.

The second category of mature student is often of more interest to the dental school selectors and interviewers. Applications from people aged under 30 who have achieved success in other careers and who can bring a breadth of experience to the dental school and to the profession are welcomed.

The main difficulty facing those who come late to the idea of studying dentistry is that they rarely have scientific backgrounds. They face the daunting task of studying science A levels and need very careful counselling before they embark on what will, inevitably, be quite a tough programme. Independent sixth-form colleges provide this counselling as part of their normal interview procedure.

STUDYING ABROAD

One option for those who have been unsuccessful with their applications is to study dentistry abroad – for example at Charles University in the Czech Republic. The course is taught in English, and graduates must then pass the International Qualifying Examination (IQE) set by the General Dental Council. Contact details are given at the end of the book.

The University of Sussex (in association with M & D Europe) also runs a pre-dentistry course, which can involve overseas study. See www.mdpremed.com.

4

DENTAL SCHOOL AND BEYOND

Dental courses are carefully planned to give the
students a wide range of academic and practical
experience, which will lead to final qualification
as a dentist. At the end of the five-year course
students will, if they have met the high academic
standards demanded, be awarded a Bachelor of
Dental Surgery (referred to as either a BDS or a
BChD, depending on which dental school you
are at).

The structure of all dental courses is similar with most
institutions offering two years of pre-clinical studies
(often undertaken with medical students at the same university) followed by three years of clinical studies. The
pre-clinical studies are often taught outside the dentistry
school with regular visits to the school forming part of
the learning programme. However, every school differs in
the way in which it delivers the material so it is very
important to get hold of, and thoroughly read, their latest
prospectuses.

Universities teach in a range of ways, from the more
traditional large lectures to small tuition groups of

approximately eight. A number of the schools, such as Liverpool and Manchester, have successfully used a problem-based learning (PBL) approach which, they feel, encourages the students to develop an independent and inquisitive approach to learning, using libraries and discussing problems with colleagues to, as the name suggests, solve problems. Some schools stress the importance of contact with the patient very early in the course whilst others prefer students to finish the pre-clinical course before this happens. All the schools are very interested in embracing the latest technologies using both computer modelling and the simulation of procedures and techniques using, for instance, a 'phantom head'.

The pre-clinical students will typically study some, or all, of the following courses: anatomy; physiology; biochemistry; oral biology; pharmacology; first aid; behavioural science and an introduction to the clinical skills that will be taught later in the course.

Students who perform well in the examinations at the end of the pre-clinical course often take up the opportunity to complete an intercalated BSc. This is normally a one-year project during which students have the opportunity to investigate a chosen topic in much more depth, producing a final written thesis before rejoining the course.

When clinical studies start, the students often take responsibility for their own patients in the in-house 'mini-practices' or as part of a team comprising students of varied experience (in some schools this includes training with chair-side assistants, dental technicians and hygienists). Students are also encouraged to participate in practitioner attachment schemes in which they spend time with General Dental Practitioners, specialist dental units and the Community Dental Service. Time can also be spent at local hospitals to gain experience of accident and emergency, general, and ear, nose and throat surgery. To teach the patient care necessary to effectively treat a whole range of people, many schools are now offering courses in behavioural sciences and the management of pain and anxiety, and in the treatment of children, the elderly and the disabled.

The clinical students will typically study some of the following courses: behavioural science; computing and statistics; dental materials; dental public health; dental prosthetics; haematology; operative technique and clinical skills; children's dentistry; restorative dentistry; oral medicine and surgery; oral pathology; oral biochemistry and biology; orthodontics; medico-legal and ethical aspects of dental practice; forensic dentistry; sedation; radiology and other aspects of the management of pain and anxiety in dentistry.

Towards the end of the course there is often the opportunity to take an elective study period, when students are expected to undertake a short project but are free to travel to any hospital or clinic in the world that is approved by their university. For example, Bristol dental school has links with, amongst others, Bordeaux, Paris and Valencia, and less formal links with other parts of the world. A number of dental schools have excellent working links with continental universities. This means that under the Socrates–Erasmus scheme a limited number of students study at another participating European university and are credited with the academic work they undertake there.

At the end of Year 5 there is a final BDS/BChD professional examination. The dental schools include all clinical aspects of dentistry in their courses, which means that graduates are competent to carry out most treatments and exercise independent clinical judgements.

CAREERS IN DENTISTRY

GENERAL DENTAL PRACTITIONERS (GDPs)

According to the British Dental Association, there are about 21,000 NHS GDPs in the UK. Some of these run dental practices on their own, whereas others work in larger practices or groups of practices. Most dental practices offer NHS and private treatment.

Some patients receive free treatment from their NHS dentists, who are then reimbursed by the government. Free treatment is given to patients falling into any (or all) of the following categories:

- Under 18-year-olds
- Under 19-year-olds who are still in full-time education
- Pregnant women
- Women with children under 12 months old
- Those on low incomes.

Private patients are offered a much wider range of treatment, but they or their dental insurance scheme providers (about one million people have private dental plans) pay the full cost, which is determined by the dentist rather than the NHS. Following graduation, there is one year of compulsory vocational training (VT). During VT, the newly graduated dentists (now known as Vocational Dental Practitioners, or VDPs) work in approved dental practices. The VDPs are paid by the NHS, and their trainers are also paid an allowance. Any earnings generated by the VDP go to the trainer. More details about VT can be found on the BDA website. Following VT, most dentists join a practice as an assistant dentist or as an associate dentist. There is a difference between assistant dentists and associate dentists. Assistant dentists are employed by the practice owner, and are paid a salary; associate dentists are self-employed, but work in a practice owned by someone else. The associate dentist buys services from the practice owner, such as nursing or technician support, materials and access to patients, either by paying the practice owner a percentage of his/her earnings, or a fixed monthly fee.

Many dentists then take the step of becoming a practice owner. This means that they run a business and are responsible not only for the treatment that they provide for their own patients, but also for the administration of the practice, and the employment of associate dentists if necessary. This is an aspect of the career that attracts many students to the profession.

CASE STUDY   Mike studied at Leeds. He had wanted to be a doctor since he was ten, but when he was trying to get hospital work experience, his own dentist suggested that Mike shadow him for a week. He immediately realised that he enjoyed dentistry work experience much more than the medical placements, and he decided to change direction.

'I don't know what it was that made me decide on dentistry rather than medicine, but I came away from the dental practice each evening feeling excited, rather than depressed as was happening when I shadowed doctors, who were all very negative about a career as a doctor. One of the things I particularly liked was how grateful the patients were, and how the dentist was able to build up a relationship with them because he saw them on a regular basis. Doctors only see sick people!'

Mike was only made one offer, of ABB. In the end, he only achieved BBB but was accepted anyway, because he had performed well at interview.

'I think it's fair to say that I made the most of my time at dental school. I played rugby and had a very good social life, as well as working very, very hard indeed. My aim is to own my own practice, somewhere in a big city. I like the idea of running a business, and I think that I would be good at it – I always enjoyed coming up with money-making schemes when I was at school.'

The British Dental Association estimates that a dentist with no private patients earns, on average, about £100,000 a year. Dentists who offer private treatment generally earn more than this. Before you begin to think about how many Ferraris you could buy when you become a dentist, you should be aware that the expenses associated with running a practice can take more than 50% of this (on, for instance, wages, materials and the practice building). Even sole practitioners, who generally have greater control over the running of a practice, cannot expect to keep more than about 60% of their income. Another factor to consider is that, unlike other careers in which earnings rise year after year, dentists often reach a peak in their 30s, and their earnings can fall after this as they become older, slower and less inclined to work long hours.

CASE STUDY

Sarah sat her A levels in Biology, Chemistry and Maths in a school in Kent, and gained grades ABB respectively. She chose King's from the three dental schools that offered her a place, because she wanted to study in London. About the course, she says, 'I enjoyed studying alongside the doctors, as they tended to be a bit more lively than the dentists. I think that they need to get it out of their systems, because when they qualify, they have very little time for a personal life, whereas being a dentist gives you more flexibility to separate work from social life.'

Sarah now works in Sussex, as an associate dentist in a practice in a small town. 'I like the fact that many of my patients live in the country, and are more interested in keeping their teeth healthy than in cosmetic dentistry – in cities, people tend to be more vain.'

Her advice for women thinking of dentistry as a career: 'You need to be physically quite strong, because you are on your feet a lot of the time, and performing extractions is hard work. In many ways it is an advantage being a woman, because children are less intimidated by you. What do I dislike about being a dentist? The way that people react when you tell them what you do – they always have a horror story to tell about their dentists when they were children. The best thing? I will be able to continue my career when I have children.'

COMMUNITY DENTAL SERVICE AND HOSPITAL DENTISTRY

Some newly qualified dentists prefer to follow a more structured (and possibly less risky) path, and choose to become part of the Community Dental Service, which provides dental treatment for patients with special needs, or to work in a hospital. Hospital dentistry concentrates on more specialist areas such as orthodontics, restorative dentistry for victims of accident or illness, paediatric dentistry or oral medicine. As a hospital dentist, the career path is similar to that followed by a doctor: House Officer, Senior House Officer and so on, up to Consultant level.

OTHER CAREERS

Dentists can also find employment in the armed services and within industry. For those with an interest in the academic aspects of dentistry, there are opportunities for research or teaching within universities.

5

CURRENT ISSUES

FLUORIDATION

What is fluoride?

Fluorine is a naturally occurring gas. When fluorine forms a binary compound with another element, this compound is known as a fluoride. Fluoride ions are found in soil, fresh water and seawater, plants and many foods. It has a beneficial effect on dental health.

How does fluoride work?

Fluoride is beneficial to both developing and developed teeth as it decreases the risk of decay. Dental decay is caused by acids produced by the plaque on our teeth which react with the sugars and other carbohydrates we eat. The acids attack the tooth enamel which, after repeated attacks, will break down, allowing cavities to form. Fluoride acts by bonding to the tooth enamel and reducing the solubility of the enamel in the acids. Fluoride also inhibits the growth of the bacteria responsible for tooth decay. There is also evidence that it helps repair the very earliest stages of decay by promoting the remineralisation of the tooth enamel. Fluoride is not a cure-all and the risk of tooth decay can still be increased by other factors such as exposed roots, frequent sugar and carbohydrate consumption, bad oral hygiene and reduced saliva flow.

How was fluoride discovered to be beneficial to dental health?
The earliest work on the benefits of fluoridation dates
from the studies of Frederick MacKay, a dentist in
Colorado in the early 1900s. MacKay noted a condition in
his patients which was previously undescribed in the liter-
ature. Many of his patients had a strange brown staining
on their teeth. Subsequent research by MacKay and a col-
league, D. V. Black, resulted in the discovery that mottled
enamel (what we now refer to as dental fluorosis) was
due to imperfections in the formation of the tooth
enamel. They also noticed that individuals with dental fluorosis had teeth that were particularly resistant to decay.
MacKay continued his research and discovered the link
between dental fluorosis and the naturally high levels of
fluoride in the drinking water in Colorado springs.

What is fluoridation?
Fluoride occurs naturally in our water supply. Fluoridation is the process by which the amount of fluoride is
adjusted to the optimum level which protects against
tooth decay. The optimum level is 1 part per million
(ppm). With few exceptions, levels in UK water supplies
are considerably lower than the optimum value.

What are the benefits of fluoridation?
Initially the main beneficiaries of fluoridated water supplies were thought to be children under the age of five
years. In areas where the concentration of fluoride in
water supplies is 1ppm, rates of decay and tooth loss in
children are greatly reduced. High levels of tooth decay in
children are generally associated with areas of social deprivation. This is a pattern repeated throughout the EU and
the US. The best dental health regions in the UK are the
West Midlands, an area where over two thirds of the population receive fluoridated water, and South East England,
which is predominantly an affluent area. The worst areas
for dental health are those associated with high levels of
social deprivation such as North West England and
Scotland. Children living in socially deprived areas which
have non- fluoridated water supplies can suffer up to six
times more tooth decay than those living in more affluent
areas or those receiving fluoridated water supplies. For
example, in the poorest communities of North West

England as many as one in three children of pre-school age have had a general anaesthetic for tooth extraction and in Glasgow tooth extraction is the most common reason for general anaesthetic for children under the age of 10.

Subsequent research has shown that it is not only children who benefit from fluoridated water supplies but people of all ages as the effect of fluoride on the surface of fully developed teeth is thought to be even more important. In particular the elderly can benefit from drinking fluoridated water. The decrease in saliva flow with age combined with reduced manual dexterity mean keeping your teeth clean as you get older is more difficult. This means the elderly are more prone to root surface decay, which is difficult to treat. As fluoride strengthens adult tooth enamel it helps reduce the incidence of this type of decay.

Probably the two most important advantages of fluoridated water supplies as opposed to any other method of combating tooth decay are that it is cost effective and, most importantly, that all members of the community are reached, regardless of income, education or access to dental care.

What are the problems with fluoridation?
One of the side effects of an excessive intake of fluoride is dental fluorosis. This is a mottling of the teeth caused by a disruption of the enamel formation of teeth whilst they are developing under the gums. This occurs from birth to the age of five. After this age the enamel is completely developed. In mild cases dental fluorosis is purely a minor cosmetic problem, which is barely visible to either the individual or the observer. It is also thought that mild dental fluorosis may further increase the resistance of the tooth enamel to decay. In moderate to severe cases of dental fluorosis colouring of the teeth is very pronounced and irregularities develop on the tooth surface. Whether this is purely cosmetic or whether it adversely affects the function of the teeth is a matter of some debate.

Some research has claimed links with higher instances of bone cancer, osteoarthritis and fractures. At present scientific studies supporting these findings are rare and they remain somewhat unsubstantiated, with the majority of scientific opinion believing there to be no link between fluoridated water supplies and these diseases.

The reasons for the varying rates of tooth decay and loss in children are complex but include the amount of sugar in their diet, the availability, affordability and use of fluoride toothpaste and the presence of fluoride in other areas of their diet eg water, milk and salt. Fluoridation of water supplies does not tackle the underlying issue of educating people in good oral hygiene and better diet.

Other concerns expressed about fluoridation are its effect on the environment, particularly on plants. Fluorides have been used in some pesticides and insecticides and their use is now restricted. Other industrial fluorides are one of the main pollutants in lakes, rivers, streams and the atmosphere.

What are the ethical issues involved in fluoridation?
One of the main issues surrounding ethical problems with fluoridation of water supplies involves infringement of personal liberty as it effectively medicates everyone without an individual having the choice to refuse. We have no choice of water supply other than what is supplied through our water company, unless we opt to buy bottled water, the cost of which would be prohibitive for certain sections of the community.

The other main issue involves weighing up whether one segment of society should benefit whilst another could potentially be put at risk. By giving fluoridated water supplies to individuals who have high intake of fluoride from other sources, they could theoretically be put at risk – but by an action that would, according to present scientific opinion, benefit thousands of deprived children.

What is the situation in the UK?
In the UK less than 10% of water supplies are fluoridated. Approximately 5.5 million people, mainly in the West Midlands and North East England, receive optimally fluoridated water.

At present in the UK, water companies can block fluoridation schemes despite health authorities' wishes. The government is intending to change the law so that water companies have to comply with the wishes of the local health authority. However, fluoridation would only be introduced following extensive publicity and public consultation.

The areas in most need of fluoridated water supplies, those with high tooth decay rates, include Merseyside and other parts of North West England, Yorkshire, Scotland, Wales and Northern Ireland plus some socially deprived communities in the South, such as Inner London.

Who supports water fluoridation in the UK?
- British Dental Association
- British Medical Association
- British Fluoridation Society
- World Health Organization.

What is the situation in other parts of the world?
The pattern of socially deprived areas having a high incidence of tooth decay has been repeated throughout the EU. Policy throughout the EU varies, with some member states having optimally fluoridated water supplies and others supporting the idea but for various reasons not having fluoridated supplies (eg Sweden and the Netherlands). The other main receivers of fluoridated water are in the US (60%) and Australia (above 65%).

What other products have fluoride added?
Several other methods of increasing fluoride intake have been used, the most obvious of which is toothpaste. Salt fluoridation has been used as an alternative to water fluoridation in several countries including Switzerland, France, Belgium, Colombia, Jamaica and Costa Rica. This has the advantage of not requiring a centralised piped water system. However, it is not without its problems: dosage must take into account the other sources of fluoride in the area, ensuring intake is not excessive. The production of fluoridated salt also requires specialist technology. Another consideration is the link between consumption of sodium and hypertension, which would make this method of fluoride intake unsuitable for some individuals.

Experiments using fluoridated milk supplies have also been carried out. So far these have been small studies in which fluoride is added to milk given to children in nursery and primary schools (tests have been carried out in Bulgaria, Russia and the UK). This would directly target children. However, absorption of fluoride from milk is thought to be slower than from water. Another problem would be monitoring and controlling fluoride administered in this manner, as it would be more difficult than with water because of the number of dairies involved. Fluoridated milk would also have to have an adjusted dosage of fluoride depending on whether the water supply was already naturally fluoridated or not. Additionally, a significant number of people do not drink milk for health or other reasons.

MERCURY FILLINGS

Amalgam fillings (often known as 'silver' fillings) – the most common type of metal fillings – contain a high proportion (about 50%) of mercury, a toxic metal. The remainder is made up of copper, tin, silver and zinc. There has always been a belief that the mercury could not escape from the mixture, but there is some evidence that mercury vapour does escape. The BDA accepts that a tiny amount may escape, but that this amount is harmless to most (97%) of the population. Some countries have banned the use of mercury in fillings, among them Sweden and Austria. Critics of mercury in fillings claim that the mercury vapour can cause gum disease, kidney, liver and lung problems, Alzheimer's disease and multiple sclerosis. The British Society for Mercury-free Dentistry recommends the removal of amalgam fillings, to be replaced by composite fillings, but only if precautions are taken to ensure that mercury is not ingested or inhaled. 'White' fillings – made of composite materials or polymers – can be used in place of silver fillings, but they are not as strong and so can often be unsuitable for back teeth which are subjected to greater stress than front teeth. Also being developed is the 'smart filling' – a filling that releases calcium and phosphate ions on contact with acids from the tooth bacteria that cause decay. These ions not only stop the decay, but also help to repair damage.

WAS MY TREATMENT NECESSARY?

On pages 4 and 53, the way in which dentists are paid was discussed. It is clear that, since dentists are paid for the treatment that they perform, the more treatment, or the more complex the treatment is, the more the dentist will earn. Whilst the great majority of dentists are scrupulous about providing only appropriate treatment, there have been well-publicised cases of dentists providing unnecessary fillings, crowns or extractions, simply to make more money. The *Guardian*, in an article headlined *'Do dentists put the bite on patients?'* (May 1999) carried out an albeit limited experiment to test this: a reporter booked examinations at a number of surgeries in London, and the recommendations ranged from one filling and a trip to the hygienist (cost £32.92) to two fillings and three replacement crowns (£915). Even bearing in mind that dentists have to use their professional judgement as to whether treatment is urgently required, or whether it could be delayed, the range of recommended treatment in this particular instance is staggering. The BDA commented on the survey by saying 'Differences in diagnosis are not unusual. It is a matter of judgement and opinion and much will depend on what the patient wants. If you saw lots of GPs you'd probably obtain lots of different diagnoses as well.' The BDA website has some useful information on the reasons why dentists sometimes disagree on the nature or the extent of treatment. Dental decay often progresses slowly and the point at which treatment becomes necessary is a matter of judgement. When a dentist decides that treatment is appropriate, there is often more than one type of treatment that is appropriate. According to the BDA, 'A dentist's advice about treatment will depend on a number of factors – whether the patient has been seen before, a dentist's understanding of a particular problem the patient might have, the patient's oral hygiene (which might make certain advanced forms of treatment less feasible), the patient's timescale, and so on.'

The new NHS reforms (see page 69) aim to reduce the amount of unnecessary treatment. The NHS undertakes checks to ensure that patients are getting appropriate treatment by asking a sample of the patients from each

NHS dentist in the UK to attend a check-up by an independent dentist to assess the amount and the quality of the treatment.

THE NATION'S TEETH

There has been a steady improvement in dental health in the UK. According to a report by the Office of Population Censuses & Surveys, in 1978, 30% of the adult population had lost all of their natural teeth, but by 1998 this figure had fallen to 13%. In 1998 adults who still had their own teeth had, on average, 15.8 sound and untreated teeth, compared with 13.0 in 1978. The average number of missing teeth fell from 9.0 in 1978 to 7.2 in 1998. The average number of decayed teeth also fell from 1.9 to 1.0.

Reasons for this improvement include:

- Fluoridation of water
- Fluoride in toothpaste
- Developments in dental treatment
- Preventative and restorative dental treatment
- Increased awareness of dental health.

In 2003, a survey into the health of children's teeth (www.statistics.gov.uk/children/dentalhealth) revealed that although the health of children's teeth is continuing to improve, there is a big gap between the best and the worst, and some of this is to do with regional differences. Professor Liz Kay, Scientific Adviser to the BDA (quoted on the BDA's website), said 'While this report does demonstrate a welcome overall improvement in children's dental health, the gulf between those with the best and worst oral health persists. This report shows that a high percentage of our children still suffer unacceptable levels of tooth decay.'

A report in the March 2004 edition of the *British Dental Journal* says that children from Asian backgrounds have healthier teeth. According to the report, over 60 per cent of white children have some tooth erosion, compared to under 50 per cent in children from Asian families. In both groups, boys were more likely to be affected than girls. The report highlights the statistical correlation between high levels of sugar in the diet and levels of tooth erosion.

Different dietary habits between the two groups, therefore, might be part of the explanation.

One of the major contributing factors towards tooth decay and erosion in children is the consumption of fizzy drinks. According to the BDA, the effect of consuming any fizzy drink increased the chance of tooth erosion in 14-year-olds by 220 per cent (and over 90 per cent of 14-year-olds drink fizzy drinks). Children who drink a number of fizzy drinks a day have a 500 per cent increase in the chance of causing damage to their teeth.

The National Institute for Clinical Excellence (NICE) published new guidelines on the recommended frequency of dental check-ups. At the moment, the recommended interval between check-ups has been the same (usually six months) regardless of the patient's age and oral health. Ralph Davies of the BDA, quoted on the BDA's website, said: '*The British Dental Association has always held that the frequency of dental check-ups should be based on the individual patient, not a "one size fits all" system. How often you need an examination should be based on what is best for you as a patient and the clinical judgement of your dentist. NICE has also called for more research to be carried out on this subject and the BDA strongly supports this.*'

The new guidelines might also help to cut the waiting lists for NHS dentists. It has been estimated that the NHS is nearly 2000 dentists short of what is needed to provide an effective oral care system in England. This shortage is predicted to rise to over 5000 by 2011, according to *The Times* (October 2004). Less than 50 per cent of adults in England have attended an NHS dentist. The government has agreed to spend over £350 million on NHS dentistry reforms and on the recruitment of 1000 new dentists.

FILLINGS COULD BE HISTORY

Over the past thirty years, our teeth have got much better. We look after them better, visit the dentist more and are more 'tooth aware'. It is now common for people over the age of 30 to boast that they've never had a filling or crown – something unheard of a generation ago. However, many people still get cavities and so drilling and filling has not gone away.

Now a new treatment promises an end to this as well. It is not (yet) widely available (a handful of private dental practices across the country use the treatment) but HealOzone could, according to its cheerleaders, banish unsightly fillings once and for all from our mouths. The treatment involves using a laser to detect tooth decay. Then the tooth is enclosed in a special airtight rubber cup and the air removed and replaced by ozone, a powerful germicide. The ozone kills the bacteria that cause decay instantly and the cavity in the tooth either 'remineralises' naturally, aided by calcium salts in your saliva, or if the hole is too big, is filled with a cosmetic white filling without the need for drilling. Remineralisation is aided by a mouthwash containing fluoride, calcium, zinc, phosphate and xylitol.

A spokesman for James Hull Associates (JHA), one of the largest chains of dental practices to offer HealOzone, reported that 'It works in 90% of cases at the first treatment. It takes 40 seconds a tooth against the half-hour process of injections, drilling and filling. Once the equipment has been purchased (about £15,000) the treatments could also prove to be cheaper than the more conventional treatments.'

The British Dental Association, whilst being impressed with some of the early results, has asked for the use of ozone in the medical field to be monitored carefully. 'It is not new, its use in the medical field extends back to before the First World War and some countries (for example Cuba) still use it very extensively. Whilst it is very useful in the upper atmosphere it is a pollutant and a major cause of smog and respiratory problems.' JHA countered by saying that each tooth is isolated within an airtight rubber cup and the treatment is so localised that there is not a problem. The Federal Food and Drugs Administration in the USA is adamant that 'ozone is a toxic gas with no known useful medical application in specific, adjunctive or preventative therapy. In order for ozone to be effective as a germicide, it must be present in a concentration far greater than that which can be safely tolerated by man.' The British Dental Association would like more research to take place and to gain assurances that ozone is not harming the mouth. They did however stress that the use of ozone was a minor issue and that the majority of a dentist's work was now preventative or cosmetic.

NHS REFORMS

In April 2006, the government introduced new systems of payment for dental treatment, and also changed the way that patients have access to NHS dentists. Under the old system, dentists were paid for each treatment they performed, and there were around 400 separate charges. The new system gives dentists a guaranteed income for providing a certain level of NHS treatment, in order to try to avoid the problem of unnecessary treatment (see page 65). The payment to dentists is calculated by looking at their income in the period before the reforms came into effect. The government argues that this will take pressure off dentists to treat patients and therefore allow them to spend more time on preventative dentistry.

Under the new system, patients pay one of four fixed charges:

1 | £15.50 for diagnosis, planning and maintenance – for instance, a check-up and descaling.
2 | £42.40 for simple treatment – fillings and extractions, for example.
3 | £189.00 for provision of appliances, such as dentures or crowns.
4 | £15.50 for emergency treatment.

The British Dental Association is not particularly happy with the reforms. A survey of dentists carried out by the BDA revealed that 55 per cent of dentists did not think that the reforms allowed them to see more patients. Before the reforms, according to the BDA, 32 per cent of dentists performed 95 per cent of their work on NHS patients, but this has fallen to 25 per cent since the reforms. Full details of the reforms can be found on the BDA website.

FURTHER INFORMATION

TABLES

TABLE 1: DENTAL SCHOOL ADMISSIONS POLICIES – 2007 ENTRY

	Standard offer	Interview policy	Retakes considered?	Retake offer	Sciences preferred
Belfast	AAA	<5%	Yes[1]	AAA	Two[6,7,8]
Birmingham	AAB	~35–40%	No	–	Two[6,7,9]
Bristol	AAB	~40%	Yes[1]	AAA	Two[8,10]
Cardiff	AAB	~40%	Yes	AAA	Two[7]
Dundee	AAA	<40%	No	–	Two[11]
Glasgow	AAB	~55%	Yes[2]	AAA	Two[6,7]
Leeds	AAB	~50%	Yes[1]	AAA	Two
Liverpool	AAB	~40%	Yes[1]	AAA	Two[7]
King's	AAB	~60%	Yes[3]	AAB	Three
Manchester	AAB	~25%	Yes[4]	AAA	Two[6,11]
Newcastle	AAB	~20%	No	–	Two[6,7]
Queen Mary	AAB	~60%	Yes[3]	AAA	Three[9]
Sheffield	AAB	~40%	Yes[5]	AAA	Two[6]

Note: All instititutions prefer candidates to have Biology and Chemistry at A level.
1 Only if you applied first time, held this offer as your first choice and achieved at least BBB.
2 Only if you applied first time, held this offer as your first choice and achieved at least BCC.
3 Only in extenuating circumstances.
4 Only if you applied first time, held this offer as your first choice, achieved at least CCC and have substantiated extenuating circumstances for this underachievement.
5 Previous application to the university is preferred.
6 Chemistry is required.
7 Two science A levels are required; three are preferred.
8 Grade A in AS level Biology is required.
9 If only one of Biology and Chemistry is taken at A level, the other is required at AS level.
10 Biology is essential if the third A level is a non-science subject. Biology should be taken to at least AS level.
11 Biology is required.

TABLE 2: DENTAL SCHOOL STATISTICS – 2005

	Applications	Interviews	Offers	Accepted
Belfast	142	<5%	70	42
Birmingham	1256	640	250	100
Bristol	664	258	204	75
Cardiff	975	180	150	67
Dundee	333	72	78	67
Glasgow	554	330	150	89
Leeds*	830	350	250	55
Liverpool	746	320	240	94
King's	1130	280	200	180
Manchester	1110	195	134	78
Newcastle	700	200	150	75
Queen Mary*	751	435	240	75
Sheffield*	867	370	256	65

* No new data available; entry data for 2004 is given.

	Clearing	Graduates	Overseas	Resits
Belfast	0	1	0	0
Birmingham	0	5	3	0
Bristol	0	6	4	5
Cardiff	0	2	3	4
Dundee	0	3	3	0
Glasgow	0	4	4	0
Leeds*	0	0	8	0
Liverpool	0	16	4	0
King's	0	15	10	0
Manchester	0	5	13	16
Newcastle	0	15	6	0
Queen Mary*	0	6	4	2
Sheffield*	0	2	0	4

* No new data available; entry data for 2004 is given.

TABLE 3: TYPICAL INTERVIEWS

	Length	Number on panel	Composition of panel	Written element?
Belfast	15 min	Three	Head of school, academic staff, academic related staff	No
Birmingham	15 min	Two	Admissions tutor plus an academic staff member	No
Bristol	20 min	Two	Clinical and non-clinical staff	10-minute exercise
Cardiff	15 min	Two	At least one senior clinician	No
Dundee	15 min	Two	Academic clinical staff	No
Glasgow	20 min	Three	Two members of admission committee (qualified dentists) and an administrator	Yes
Leeds	15 min	Two	One academic and one senior administrator	No
Liverpool	15 min	Two	Members of academic staff and local GDPs	No
King's	20 min	Two	Admissions tutor plus another academic	Questionnaire and ethical case study
Manchester	15 min	Two/three	Members of clinical and non-clinical teaching staff	No
Newcastle	20 min	Two	Senior members of academic staff (at least one clinician)	No
Queen Mary	15 min	Three	One academic, one clinician and one student	No
Sheffield	15 min	Two	One clinician member of staff and a second from another department or a community dentist	No

**FURTHER
READING**

An essential starting point is the British Dental
Association's website (www.bda.org.). This carries careers
information for prospective dentists as well as press
releases and discussion of topical issues. The BDA's websites for dental patients (www.bdasmile.org and
bda-findadentist.org.uk) are also useful.

The BDA has its own museum, the BDA Dental Museum.
Details can be found at www.bda.org/museum. An enter-
taining (and informative) site is www.3dmouth.org which
contains, as the name suggests, a computer-generated
three-dimensional mouth.

The BDA publishes a journal for dentists, the *British
Dental Journal*. Again, details of this appear on the BDA
website. The journal is aimed at practising dentists, and
can be very technical. More accessible is *Launchpad*, the
BDA's magazine for dental students and newly qualified
dentists.

Dentistry (www.dentistry.co.uk) is an independent dental
magazine published every fortnight. It carries news, clinical articles, business articles, education features and
product information.

To keep up to date with dentistry and dental issues in the
UK, the *Independent*, the *Guardian*, the *Daily Telegraph* and
The Times all carry regular health reporting, and have
health sections once a week. The Sunday broadsheet
papers often contain summaries of medicine or dentistry-
related issues.

Another source of dental news is the website
www.topix.net/business/dental, which covers topical
dentistry stories from the UK and worldwide.

For information on grade requirements, *Degree Course
Offers*, written by Brian Heap and published by Trotman
(www.trotman.co.uk, Tel: 020 8486 1150), or the *UCAS
Big Guide* (UCAS, Tel: 01242 222444).

If you are thinking of studying dentistry overseas, M & D
Europe is a good source of information. It aims to help
you get a place on a course taught in English – and, once

you have qualified, to help you get placements at hospitals in the UK. Its website, www.readmedicine.com, gives details of dental schools in the Czech Republic and the Cayman Islands.

The International Society for Fluoride Research publishes its own journal called *Fluoride*. Some articles from the journal are available on the Society's website www.fluoride-journal.com

Queen Mary's *Rough Guide to Dentistry* can be accessed on its website at www.qmul.ac.uk/medicineanddentistry

www.admissionsforum.net is a chatroom for potential medical and dental applicants.

CONTACT DETAILS

ORGANISATIONS

British Dental Association
64 Wimpole Street
London W1M 8AL
Tel 0207 935 0875
www.bda.org

British Fluoridation Society
4th Floor
School of Dentistry
University of Liverpool
Liverpool L69 3BX
bfs@liv.ac.uk

British Medical Association
BMA House
Tavistock Square
London WC1H 9JP
Tel: 020 7387 4499
www.bma.org.uk

General Dental Council
37 Wimpole Street
London W1G 8DQ
Tel: 020 7887 3800
www.gdc-uk.org

DENTAL SCHOOLS

Belfast
Dr Donald Burden
Head of Dentistry
Queen's University
Grosvenor Road
Belfast BT12 6BP
Tel: 028 9063 2733
Fax: 028 9042 8861
www.qub.ac.uk/cd

Birmingham
Mr Donald Spence
Admissions Tutor
School of Dentistry
University of Birmingham
St Chad's Queensway
Birmingham B4 6NN
Tel: 0121 237 2766
Fax: 0121 237 2932
www.dentistry.bham.ac.uk

Bristol
Dr Karen Duncan
Dental School
University of Bristol
Lower Maudlin Street
Bristol BS1 2LY
Tel: 0117 928 4355
Fax: 0117 928 4150
www.dentalschool.bris.ac.uk

Cardiff
Mrs Lindsay J Thompson
Admissions Officer
Dental School
Cardiff University
Heath Park
Cardiff CF14 4XN
Tel: 029 2074 4277/25
Fax: 029 2077 6343
www.cardiff.ac.uk/dentistry

Dundee
Gordon Black
Medicine/Dentistry Admissions Officer
University of Dundee
Park Place
Dundee DD1 4HN
Tel: 01382 384032
Fax: 01382 225163
www.dundee.ac.uk/dentalschool

Glasgow
Miss Helen-Marie Clayton
Glasgow Dental Hospital and School
378 Sauchiehall Street
Glasgow G2 3JZ
Tel: 0141 211 9703/4
Fax: 0141 331 2798
www.gla.ac.uk/schools/dental

King's College London
Dr A M Skelly
Guy's, King's & St Thomas' Dental Institute
King's College London
Hodgkin Building
Guy's Campus
London SE1 1UL
Tel: 020 7848 6512
Fax: 020 7848 6510
www.kcl.ac.uk/depsta/dentistry

Leeds
Mrs Lesley Aitken
Leeds Dental Institute
Leeds University
Clarendon Way
Leeds LS2 9LU
Tel: 0113 343 6169
Fax: 0113 343 6165
www.leeds.ac.uk/dental

Liverpool
Dr AJ Preston
Admissions Tutor
School of Dentistry
University of Liverpool
Pembroke Place
Liverpool L3 5PS
Tel: 0151 706 5298
Fax: 0151 706 5652
www.liv.ac.uk/dental

Manchester
Mrs Teresa Smith
Undergraduate Admissions (BDS)
Dean's Administrative Offices
University Dental Hospital of Manchester
Higher Cambridge Street
Manchester M15 6FH
Tel: 0161 275 6603
Fax: 0161 275 6604
www.den.man.ac.uk

Newcastle
Mrs L O'Connor
School Administrator
School of Dental Sciences
Framlington Place
Newcastle University
Newcastle upon Tyne NE2 4BW
Tel: 0191 222 8347
Fax: 0191 222 6137
www.ncl.ac.uk/dental

Peninsula College of Medicine and Dentistry
Admissions Tutor
Peninsula Dental School
John Bull Building
Tamar Science Park
Research Way
Plymouth
PL6 8BU
Tel: 01752 437333
Fax: 01752 517842
www.pms.ac.uk

Queen Mary (Barts and the London)
Dr Chris Mercer
St Bartholomew's and the Royal London School
  of Medicine and Dentistry
Turner Street
London E1 2AD
Tel: 020 7377 7611
Fax: 020 7377 7612
www.smd.qmul.ac.uk/dental

Sheffield
Mrs Amanda Okrasa
Admissions Secretary
School of Clinical Dentistry
Claremont Crescent
Sheffield S10 2TA
Tel: 0114 271 7808
Fax: 0114 279 7050
www.shef.ac.uk/dentalschool

POSTSCRIPT

If you have any comments or questions arising out of this book, I would be very happy to answer them. You can contact me at the address given below.

Good luck with your application to dental school!

James Burnett

If you have any questions about your application to dental school, please contact me at:

MPW
90–92 Queen's Gate
London
SW7 5AB
Tel: 020 7835 1355
Fax: 020 7259 2705

BURNING
SHIPS

JOHN STEELE

&

NOREEN STEELE

Argyll
publishing

First Published 1996
Argyll Publishing
Glendaruel
Argyll PA22 3AE
Scotland

The two close friends of the authors who survived the
traumatic ordeal at sea expressed a wish not to be
named. This wish has been respected by the use of
pseudonyms.

British Library Cataloguing-in-Publication Data.
A catalogue record for this book is available from the
British Library.

ISBN 1 874640 62 9

Origination
Cordfall Ltd, Glasgow

Printing
Caledonian International
Book Manufacturing, Glasgow

to our grandchildren,
Robbie, Kirsten, Campbell,
Blair, Findlay and little Sarah,
who are a constant source of joy to Gran and Papa

CONTENTS

ACKNOWLEDGEMENTS

Among many others we would like to acknowledge the invaluable assistance of the following in preparing the book.

Danish Maritime Museum,

Ian Douglas, Dumfries,

HM Coastguard, Bangor,

HM Coastguard, Clyde MRCC,

HM Coastguard, Southampton,

Captain Ted Fields, Maritime Safety Consultant, Glasgow (0141 943 0256)

Dipl. Ing Karl-Werner and Maria Fischer, Kassel, Germany,

Combined Operations Museum, Inverary, Argyll,

Commander R Kirkwood, Royal Navy,

John Linton, Ardrossan,

MAIB Southampton,

CA Mair (Shipping) Ltd, Ardrossan, Royal Norwegian Vice Consul and Royal Danish Vice Consul,

Marine Safety Agency, Glasgow,

Marine Safety Agency, Southampton,

Captain A Murchie, Ardrossan,

NUMAST London,

Scottish Daily Mail,

Scottish Maritime Museum, Irvine,

Sea Breezes,

Shipping Today & Yesterday,
Ships Monthly,
State Marine Information Centre, Wilhelmshaven,
Jim Stephen, Sumas USA,
Strathclyde Fire Brigade,
Brian Wilson MP, Shadow Transport Spokesman.

John Steele and Noreen Steele
Ardrossan, Scotland
May 1996

FOREWORD

The newsworthiness of accidents and disasters tend not
be measured by the number of casualties. So the fire on
board the *Tor Scandinavia* in 1989, in which just two people
died, was soon overtaken by other events and more
numerically impressive tragedies.

Only those caught up in the drama knew how much
worse it could have been. And for two of the passengers
on board, John and Noreen Steele, it was not just a
terrifying experience which could be put to one side as a
grim memory. They were determined that vital lessons
should be learnt.

As an experienced firefighter, John Steele was not only
caught up in the life-saving drama which is so vividly
described in these pages. He was also in a position to
recognise the shortcomings in the ship's safety arrangements and to realise that, unless these were addressed,
other vessels would remain vulnerable to the same
dangers.

I first became familiar with the story when, as the
Steeles' constituency MP, I was asked to help ensure a full
and adequate inquiry by the Danish authorities. While
much more responsible than some maritime states, the
Danes' reaction was tempered by a desire not to stir up
too much fuss, which might embarrass their cruise liner
industry.

Yet as John and Noreen Steele point out, fires aboard ships are by no means uncommon — and each one has the potential to cause large numbers of casualties. The people who travel by sea, whether as a means of public transport or for pleasure, are entitled to expect a lot more from the safety regime on board many vessels.

By highlighting that fact, *Burning Ships* performs a significant public service. As shipping lines increasingly look to flags-of-convenience and low-paid crews, there is urgent need for heightened safety standards and more frequent inspections. Just as some of the grandest hotels have the dirtiest kitchens, so the story of the *Tor Scandinavia* confirms that even the smartest ships can conceal hidden dangers.

On another level, the book provides an account of the incident itself which communicates with stunning effect the complexities and dangers of a fire rescue operation.

Brian Wilson MP
House of Commons
May 1996

1

BURNING SHIP

We and our two friends Alice and Ron set off eagerly that morning in September 1989 anticipating the overnight cruise aboard a comfortable passenger ship to Sweden. Our planned stay in a luxury chalet at the holiday village of Klitterbin was just as enticing. As the car sped down the motorway, in good time to catch our sailing to Gothenberg, we were in good sprits.

The *Tor Scandinavia* looked very impressive berthed at Harwich. Its all-white colour scheme seemed to enhance the ship's size and it looked quite majestic. No time was lost in driving onboard, overnight bags were at the ready and we made haste, seeking out our allotted cabin, then all the delights in store during the cruise.

A very pleasant evening followed, the entertainment was good and we all danced till the early hours while sharing a bottle of champagne. The next day the sea was calm and it was sunny. This made a perfect start to our holiday.

After the ship berthed at Gothenberg, a leisurely two hour drive took us to our picturesque destination. It was so beautiful, the luxury log cabins were set among the trees. Adjacent to each was a full log store.

Bicycles appeared to be the common mode of

transport. So not to be outdone, bicycles were hired and the intrepid four set off for days of sightseeing.

On reaching a lovely beach we would decide to stop and picnic by the seaside. We had even managed a visit to beautiful Copenhagen. Each evening, we returned to a blazing log fire in our chalet.

The holiday passed all too soon, but as we set off for Gothenberg, on our return journey, we all looked forward eagerly to the sea crossing. The weather was warm and the sea was calm when we joined the queue of cars on the quayside, waiting to board the *Tor Scandinavia* once again.

The Scandinavian Seaways passenger-cargo vessel *Tor Scandinavia* was an imposing sight when viewed from the dock side. She departed from Gothenburg on Tuesday September 24, 1989. It was a tranquil late summer evening as the ship slipped her moorings and set sail on the twenty six hour voyage to Harwich.

The deck was lined with passengers happily taking pictures as the ship glided past the many small islands on its passage to the North Sea. Others took advantage of the comfortable seating beside the large viewing windows, whilst enjoying a snack or refreshment from the well-stocked, self-service coffee shop. There were many activities to keep everyone occupied. Names were being taken for a talent competition to be held later in the evening. Quiz forms were handed out with the clues to the answers distributed round the ship. A full range of facilities was on hand including a shopping arcade, cinema and even a sauna. The passengers could choose to dine in various restaurants.

After dinner the bars filled with the happy relaxed passengers and some prepared to dance the night away to the vibrant tunes of a highly professional six-piece band. As the night wore on, the passengers started to retire to their cabins. By midnight, the disco and the night club were in full swing. By 1am both closed down and the revellers made their way to their cabins.

The sea was calm and there was very little wind as the ship made her way to Harwich. All was quiet as the passengers and the by now, off-duty captain slept peacefully. At 4am, Chief Officer Pelle Orsted made his way to the bridge to relieve First Officer Morten Selas, who had been on duty since midnight.

The chief officer was now in command of *Tor Scandinavia*. He noted that the ship's speed was 24 knots, the weather was clear and traffic in the surrounding area was light.

Suddenly and for no reason that Pelle Orsted was aware of, at 4.55 am, the fire alarm panel in the bridge activated. The chief officer studied the alarm panel which indicated a fire in Section 23. This section comprised the forward area on deck 4 and deck 5. He attempted to reset the alarm with no success and he then sent the duty seaman Peter Olsen below deck to find out what was wrong.

As Peter Olsen made his way down to deck 4 and deck 5 he was met with a cloud of smoke at deck 8 and could go no further. Using his portable radio he notified the bridge that the ship was on fire.

The chief officer immediately went over to the alarm panel and activated the crew alarm. He then left the bridge momentarily while he went to his own cabin near-by, to get his own fire fighting kit. He returned to the bridge and activated the passenger alarm and the general alarm. He then had to leave the bridge because the dense smoke had already made it impossible to breath.

Captain Thomassen was fast asleep in his cabin when the crew alarm sounded. He quickly dressed and made his way to the crew corridor but had to drop to his knees on encountering heavy smoke. His thoughts were for the other 680 people on board. On this trip *Tor Scandinavia* was carrying 539 passengers. She had 138 crew on board as well as 3 relatives of crew members.

Slowly he crawled along the corridor then up the stairs to the bridge. Between the crew corridor and the stair there was a fire door. He noticed that it was open and when he started up the stairs he did not close it behind him. On entering the bridge his chief officer briefed him on a situation that was looking very serious.

At this point, the smoke in the bridge was so dense that both the captain and the chief officer had to leave the bridge to breath in the fresh air and to take note of the sea and wind conditions. On re-entering the bridge, the captain altered the ship's course to ensure that the smoke would cause the least trouble. He also reduced speed to 8 knots.

Below deck, the passengers were donning warm clothing and quickly making their way to safety. The crew were proceeding to their respective stations – some to the fire muster stations, some to evacuate passengers. Every member of the crew in a fire emergency has a particular part to play.

However something was wrong, badly wrong and to make matters worse, if that were possible, no one on the ship was aware of the dire straights of approximately 60 passengers. For them, no alarm sounded and no emergency announcements were heard. They were all sound asleep. The sleeping passengers were all in deck 5 forward section, blissfully unaware of the dramatic events taking place aboard ship.

Prior to the crew alarm being sounded, Radio Officer Kristen Kjaergaard was in his cabin fast asleep. He wakened just before 5am, to the sound of voices shouting and the noise of people running around in the crew corridor. The voices were shouting, "Smoke, there is smoke everywhere." At first he did not react to the disturbance. However thirty seconds later he did react to the fire alarm sounding. His duty in an emergency was in the radio room.

The radio officer got up, dressed and opened his cabin door. The corridor was filled with black smoke. There was no way he could survive in the corridor. He quickly re-entered his cabin and closed the door. He was in a life threatening situation and he decided to try once more to make his escape along the corridor. However as soon as he opened his cabin door, once more the dense black smoke drove him back inside.

Taking stock of the situation, he went over to the cabin window and saw some of the crew on the deck. He managed to attract their attention and they shouted, "Smash the window, smash the window." He sized up the situation he was in and decided to heed the advice from the crew on the deck. He then took hold of a heavy tool and started to smash the armoured glass onto the floor of the deck. After crawling out of the window, he made his way to the smoke filled bridge.

On reporting to the captain, he was ordered to make his way to the radio room and send out Mayday messages. When the radio officer explained that it was impossible to reach the radio room, the captain then told him to try the VHF radio in the bridge. The disadvantage with the VHF (very high frequency radio) lay in the fact that its range is only 30 to 50 nautical miles, depending on weather conditions. But he was able to send the following message:

MAYDAY MAYDAY MAYDAY.
TOR SCANDINAVIA, TOR SCANDINAVIA, TOR SCANDINAVIA,
OUR POSITION IS 100 MILES WEST OF ESJBERG.
PASSENGER SHIP ON FIRE.
681 PERSONNEL ON BOARD.
IMMEDIATE HELP REQUESTED.

There was silence on the bridge. The question on the minds of the captain and the radio officer was, had the signal been received? They waited. No one spoke. They looked at each other. It was the longest few moments of their lives before an acknowledgement was received, then another and another. On these busy North Sea shipping lanes the contacts kept coming. The first was from the German vessel MS *Poseidon* then *Dana Maxima*, *Dana Anglia*, *Tor Britannia*, a Russian freighter and many more vessels as well as the drilling platform *Gorm Charlie*.

All the vessels began changing course and sailing at full speed to the aid of the burning ship.

2

SHAKEN OUT OF SLEEP

The fire was raging out of control. The smoke started to creep along deck five and slowly it made its way forward, towards the sleeping passengers. Everywhere throughout the ship, passengers and crew were hurrying to the safety of the outside decks. All were completely unaware that the fire had destroyed all the service cables which served deck five. These emergency cables were for the alarm system and the public address system. They had been fitted in the ceiling area, in what was known as the Blue Hall and they were now useless.

The ingredients for a disaster were now in place – a fire out of control and 60 passengers asleep in their cabins with the smoke and flames spreading towards them.

Help however, was coming to them in the shape of one of the catering crew. It was the catering crew who formed the evacuation team and one of them was making her way to deck 5, to evacuate the passengers.

Fate however was to play another cruel part in this tragedy. When the member of the evacuation team reached deck 5 and saw the smoke and flames, she unfortunately lost control of her feelings and was found some time later, crying her heart out. She, like some others in the evacuation team, did not have a two-way radio to allow communication with those in overall control.

The passengers in deck 5 forward section slept on. The smoke was penetrating throughout the corridor. The forgotten passengers were unaware of the high drama being played in every part of the ship.

Below them was the car deck, if the fire should reach the cars and their petrol tanks, all would be lost.

I was sharing Cabin 5310 with my wife Noreen and our two friends, (writes John Steele). I will never forget Noreen shaking me out of my sleep and saying, "John, the ship is on fire."

Wakened from sleep at the end of a relaxing holiday, after a pleasant evening spent dancing with a couple of drinks, it's the kind of message that's hard to digest right away. Whether it was the tone of Noreen's voice or my conditioning in fire fighting, something in me clicked and I immediately leapt out of bed and ran out the door.

Turning right I looked down the corridor and saw the dreaded smoke swirling towards me. I remembered a young English couple who were directly opposite our cabin. They had a young baby who would be in the greatest of danger from the penetrating smoke. I knocked loudly on their door and when the young man opened it, I said, "The ship is on fire, you will have to leave now." His wife quickly covered the baby in a blanket and he asked me, "Which way will we go?"

I sensed that it was impossible for them to escape by way of the two corridors. Due to the smoke, they would have no chance of survival. However beside us was another door. There was a large notice on the door which stated Crew Only. Taking control of the situation, I instructed them to make their way to safety by means of this door.

Noreen came out of the cabin and turned to the left. "Everybody is sleeping," I said. "We will have to waken them," I shouted to her as she made her way through the smoke to alert and evacuate the sleeping passengers on the port-side of deck 5.

I made my way down the starboard corridor and I knocked on each door and waited until it was opened. "The ship is on fire, you will have to leave *now*," was the message I gave to every sleepy face.

As I proceeded down the smoke-filled corridor, I was joined by our two friends who assisted me in the mass evacuation.

As soon as the passengers were alerted, they would ask, "Which way?" My friends and I would calm them and then direct them to safety. By this time, I was perplexed as to why the crew had not made an appearance at the scene, to assist in the evacuation. No crew and no fire-fighters?

As the three of us worked our way along the smoke-filled corridor alerting passengers, we continually pressed the alarm buttons on the cabins. This would surely alert the crew. But no-one appeared to be coming to our assistance. It was a nightmare situation. We were on our own.

Knocking on some doors, other doors would open and people would ask what all the commotion was about. I explained, "The ship is on fire. For goodness sake, do not start packing. Just get out, *now!*"

I was pleased that everybody was responding to my instructions without hesitation. As one of the cabin doors opened, a young Swedish girl, about seventeen years old, asked, "What will we do?" I told her to quickly put on warm clothes and get out. A few seconds later she and her

21

friend came up to me out of the smoke. They were very frightened and both were in tears. One of the girls stood in front of me and clutched both my arms. "Which way? Which way do we go?" she asked urgently. She was becoming hysterical and given the circumstances I could not blame her.

They could not see any means of escape because of the smoke. Thoughts were flashing through my mind. After twenty three years as a fire-fighter I was thinking of the fire, the threatening smoke, the acrid taste, the sleeping passengers, no back-up, no breathing apparatus, no evacuation crew. I knew that we had all the ingredients of a disaster.

"Which way? Which way?" The young Swedish girl had a vice-like grip on my arms. I said quietly but forcefully, "Stop!" She stopped asking which way and I managed to prise her fingers from both my arms and led them both to the door that would lead them to safety.

By this time the smoke in the corridor was very black and there was that acrid taste. I knew what this acrid taste meant. It meant cables were burning. We knew it was very dangerous for us to be in the smoke-filled corridor without breathing apparatus and we followed the single line of passengers up the stairway which was marked Crew Only.

On reaching the open deck, it was such a relief to breath in the fresh air. As I stood still gulping in the cool night air, I decided to return to deck 5 as there was a strong possibility of some passengers still asleep. I turned and re-entered the stairway to make my way into the smoke.

At this point I had a feeling of great despondency that in all my years of fire fighting I had never had. I felt that I was walking to my death. It was a feeling that stayed with me as I stepped down the winding staircase. It was with me as I very slowly made my way along the corridor back to the last cabin door that I had knocked.

What if there was no one left in the cabins? Had I made the right decision? Feeling very much on my own, with no breathing apparatus, I was beginning to feel dejected at the dangerous situation I was in.

I started to knock on as many doors as I could. About ten people responded and I urgently directed them to the door that would lead them to safety. I was beginning to feel weak. I was aware of the smell of electric cables burning and the smoke had filled the corridor to almost floor level. For my own safety I knew I would have to retire to the upper deck.

I slowly made my way up the winding staircase. Each step was taking me nearer to the fresh air that my lungs were gasping for. At last I stepped onto the open deck and grasped hold of the rail, gulping for breath. As I breathed in the fresh air, I looked at the star-filled sky and the calm sea. How peaceful the scene looked, until I saw the smoke belching from mid-ship.

Beside me was a stairway leading to the bridge. Without hesitation, I bounded up the stairs, two at a time and entered the bridge. Here I saw one person. It was the captain speaking in Danish into a microphone. I waited about one and a half minutes until he finished speaking. As he looked at me, I informed him that I had fire fighting experience. He replied that he was Captain Thomassen and asked if I would assist in the fire fighting. I replied, "Of course."

3

FIRE FIGHTING

I followed Captain Thomassen to the top of the stairs outside the bridge and he directed me to the fire control area in the hallway on the deck below. I quickly reached the fire control area, where seven of the crew were grouped together. Four of them were wearing breathing apparatus and speaking in Danish.

As I approached them, they stopped speaking and looked at me. I was wearing my pyjama trousers, a loose fitting T-shirt and I was still bare footed, the same way I was dressed when Noreen had wakened me just a short time before. It all seemed so long ago.

Dressed like that, I was not surprised the firefighting team were looking me up and down. Before they started to converse again, I told them that the captain had sent me to them as I had many years fire fighting experience. Immediately the officer in charge of the fire fighting team ordered one of them to remove his breathing apparatus and give it to me.

I checked it and immediately strapped it on with the help of one of the team. A discussion then took place in Danish. After a few seconds, I said that they should speak in English and the officer in charge agreed. This officer was Chief Officer Pelle Orsted.

After a few more seconds of discussion on how we should tackle the raging fire, it was agreed that Chief Officer Orsted and I should work as a team. We would enter the port corridor and the other two fire fighters would enter the starboard corridor. The four of us were well aware that both corridors were completely smoke logged.

As we made our way to our respective positions, we adjusted our face masks, then we rechecked the gauge on our apparatus. They all read full. This equipment would mean the difference between life and death to us and it was very important that everything should be absolutely perfect – air bottles full, face mask on, with a smoke tight fit and all straps secure.

I stood at the port side door with the chief officer behind me. We looked towards the other team at the starboard door. I nodded to them and in we went.

The smoke was so thick, that if you held your hand in front of you, it could not be seen. We inched our way forward. I was holding the fully charged fire hose at the ready. The heat was tremendous but there were no flames to be seen.

As we very slowly made our way forward we kept tripping over suitcases and bags discarded by the fleeing passengers. The heat was building up causing the paint flakes from the ceiling to fall onto my bare head. I turned on the hose and scooped some of the cold water onto my hair.

The first cabin door we reached, we banged on it, then we opened it to make sure that there was no one trapped. It was empty and so we continued on our dark journey, with the hose spraying 100 gallons every minute. There was no fear felt from the ship's chief officer or myself. As there was a possibility of people still trapped in their cabins, we had to find them and evacuate them.

We progressed very slowly, edging our way forward,

banging loudly on each cabin door. Suddenly a door opened and two frightened faces appeared. Then another door opened, then another. A total of seven passengers were still trapped in this section.

What a nightmare to be in, I thought. How could a team of four fight this inferno? Here I was dressed in pyjama trousers, no protective clothing and no helmet or boots. I remembered some of the many very dangerous fires I had been involved in, but then there had been tremendous back-up and support from my colleagues in Strathclyde Fire Brigade. How stupid this situation was! Where was help to come from as the nearest land was a hundred miles away? Here I was in a smoke-filled corridor, on board a ship with a major fire burning out of control.

We had to evacuate these very frightened passengers to safety. I turned the hose off and put it on the floor. "Follow the hose and keep together," I shouted. Everyone did as I commanded. We shuffled slowly along the corridor. "Hold your breath and keep going," I shouted.

They could hardly make out what I was saying as my mask was still on my face. "Be very careful. There are suitcases lying about the floor." The chief officer calmed one of them who was very distressed about the situation we were in, but we reached the end of the corridor and counted everyone through the door. We had saved our small flock but were there any more? We held on to the hose line and retraced our steps.

The water swirling about the floor was quite warm. I of course, could feel it with my bare feet. This meant that we were approaching the seat of the fire. The cold water pouring from our hose was having little or no effect on the hot metal surfaces.

Just then, the warning whistle on my breathing apparatus activated. This meant that I had very little oxygen left and I would have to make my way out of the fire area and replace the oxygen bottle.

It is a rule that when this happens, both fire fighters keep together. So, once more I laid the fire hose on the floor and we both made our way out of the corridor. On the way we again checked all the cabins and they were empty.

At the end of the corridor, we opened the door and entered into the main hallway, firmly closing the corridor door behind us. We took off our breathing apparatus and looked for the spanner that was needed to loosen the retaining nut on the air bottle. No spanner was available and valuable minutes were lost while a crewman went to look for the vitally needed spanner.

As we replaced our respective oxygen bottles, I felt a tap on my shoulder. On looking round, there stood the fire fighter who had been ordered to give me his breathing apparatus. He spoke in Danish, I could not understand. But he pointed to his fire boots then he pointed at my feet. "Thank you," I said, as he pulled off his boots and gave them to me. They were far too big but in this situation, it was better to have boots that are too big than no boots at all.

After Chief Officer Pelle Orsted and I checked the air gauge on our breathing apparatus, we re-entered the corridor, carefully closing the door behind us, to ensure that as little smoke as possible would spread to other parts of the ship. Our action also meant that the corridor was filling up with more and more smoke. I took note that the emergency lighting system and exit signs were at ceiling level and were obscured by the smoke, thus making them ineffective.

As we very slowly felt our way along the corridor we could feel the intense heat. It was almost unbearable. The discarded suitcases were once more hampering our progress. However, on reaching the end of the hose I quickly opened up the nozzle and the water came surging out.

Once more, we inched our way forward, dragging the heavy hose with us until we reached a sliding door which was very hot. As we sprayed the water onto the door to cool it down, the hot paint flakes from the ceiling were still falling onto my bare head and at times I was shouting out, as it was quite painful. I kept scooping handfuls of water and cooling my head down. After having sprayed a great deal of water onto the door, to cool it down, we tried to slide it open. But we found it to be jammed and it would not move. The tremendous heat had buckled the door.

Using all our strength, both of us managed to slide the door open by about four inches (100mm). Beyond that, it would move no further.

That very small opening allowed us to look through and see the metal glowing bright red. For the first time we could see the inferno – this was the heart of the fire. It was roaring up what I thought was an open shaft. Little did I realise this had been a main stairway and now it was gone, consumed by the fire. What a sight! During all my fire fighting experience I had never seen anything like this. It was similar to a huge gas burner roaring. The flames were soaring up, the heat was tremendous and the noise, created inside what had been a stairway, sounded like a train thundering through a tunnel.

My fire fighting partner and I pointed the jet of water through the gap in the door way and poured hundreds of gallons of water onto the fire. As we stood shoulder to shoulder, holding the hose, we were being enveloped in black smoke and white smoke. The metal panels inside the stairwell were glowing.

What a sight it must have been – me with my pyjama trousers, a T-shirt and a pair of boots at least two sizes too big, absolutely soaked from the sweat and the water from the hose. If the circumstances had been different, it would have looked like a comedy show.

But this was no comedy. The situation was real and life threatening. The *Tor Scandinavia* was on fire and the fire was completely out of control. As for me, I was supposed to be on holiday!

These thoughts were going through my mind as the two of us remained at our post, not moving, holding the hose tightly and pointing the powerful jet of water through the small gap which we had created at the doorway. Although a hundred gallons of water a minute is a vast amount, it was having no visible impact on the fire. The flames roared and the temperature remained alarmingly high.

As we stood there, the conversation between the chief officer and I was about the ship. As we spoke to each other, the sound of our voices was distorted because of the breathing apparatus masks. But when I asked him when he had joined this ship and where he came from, I managed to make out that he had been on about eighteen months and that he came from the Faroe Isles.

As we spoke the breathing apparatus warning whistle activated. "We will have to go out again," Pelle said. By now, we were on first name terms.

We jammed the hose into the gap and left the water gushing from it into the flames and we once more made our way along the corridor. By now we were beginning to know where the discarded luggage was lying.

Once a warning whistle is activated, it remains on. The shrill whistle was with us all the way, past the cabin doors, some of which were open. The corridor seemed to be endless as we slowly made our way again to the hallway. As we stepped into relative safety, we once more closed the door behind us, took off our breathing apparatus sets and replaced the oxygen bottles.

As I was strapping on my breathing apparatus I felt another tap on my shoulder. Standing beside me was the crewman who had given me his boots. This time he gave me his fire helmet. As we had no common language I put my hand on his shoulder and said, "Thank you."

Prior to re-entering the corridor I told Pelle that we must attempt to get through the buckled sliding door. We had to get past it to reach the heart of the fire. It was imperative to get as close as possible to the inferno if we were to bring it under control.

Chief Officer Pelle Orsted shouted out a command in Danish. Immediately, one of the crew ran off and returned very quickly with the biggest crowbar I had ever seen. As he handed it to me, he also held the door open to allow us both to enter the darkened corridor for the third time.

Once more we followed the hose. As we came across a discarded case in the dark corridor, we would stop and push it to the side. Nearing the jammed sliding door, we could hear the roar of the fire. On reaching it I put the heavy crowbar into the gap and tried with all my strength to lever the door open. I tried and tried but the door did not move one inch.

Pelle said, "Let us both try." He took hold of the crowbar and we pushed together. I could see the sweat trickling down his face in the tremendous heat. At last, the door started to move. Very slowly the gap became wider and wider, until we could direct the water from our hose onto the very heart of the fire. This was it, we were in a perfect position to fight and beat our enemy.

As we stood there, holding firmly onto the hose, I had a great feeling. There is nothing better when fighting a fire, than to know that in time, we will win. We will conquer this raging fire. We had everything now on our side. We had an endless supply of water being pumped from the sea and we had the time. All we had to do was remain where we were and pour the water onto the fire. The metal plates were glowing white and red, the smoke was pouring past us and the heat was like a furnace but we were winning.

Through the smoke we could see movement. Opposite us, something was moving. Pelle and I peered and peered, then Pelle said, "It is the other two fire fighters, the two crewmen who entered the starboard corridor." We could not speak to them across the large void, as it is impossible to shout and be heard at a distance when you are wearing a breathing mask. Pelle and I were very relieved and happy that we could see them. They had made it, like us, to the most advantageous position to fight and beat the fire which was raging out of control.

Now we had two teams, each pumping 100 gallons of water per minute onto the inferno. At this point all we could do was maintain this position until our oxygen supply was depleted. We stood our ground amidst the black swirling smoke and intense heat.

Although we could make out the faint outline of the other two fire fighters, through the flames, it was impossible to make contact.

When the whistle on my breathing apparatus activated Pelle and I reluctantly had to make our way back along the corridor, back to the smoke free hallway, where we could once more replace our air bottles. As we moved slowly in the corridor, away from the fire, there were no more suitcases to fall over.

On reaching the safety of the hallway, speed was essential. We had to replace our air bottles and get back in as soon as possible.

I quickly took off my breathing apparatus and laid it on the floor. Then kneeling down beside it I removed my almost empty air bottle and looked around for a full one.

But there was none to be seen! I looked at Pelle and he said, "There are no more full air bottles on the ship but there is a ship coming to our assistance. They have a supply of full air bottles."

"When will the ship reach us," I asked, in astonishment. "In ten minutes," was the answer.

I looked at a clock on the wall. The time was half past six. I had been fighting the fire for one and a half hours. We were beating it but not now. With no breathing apparatus we could not re-enter the corridor to fight the fire. What an almighty cock up. For ten minutes the fire would rage out of control!

The ship had a total of 681 people on board. All our lives were very seriously at risk and we had no breathing apparatus to fight the fire. As I could do nothing further, I decided that as I had not seen my wife for the past one and a half hours, I would go and try and find her.

I said to Pelle, "I am going to look for my wife." He replied, "You have done very well. I do not know what I would have done without you. Thank you for all you have done." At that, we shook hands and I walked away. I was really quite dejected for two reasons. First, because of the most unhappy state of affairs we were in, with no air bottles to fight the fire; the second reason was much more important to me, as not only had I not seen Noreen for the past one and a half hours, but also during that time, I had not as much as thought of her!

4

THE SEARCH

As I made my way around the ship, looking for Noreen, I was barely aware that I was still in my night attire of pyjama trousers and a T-shirt. Both were soaking wet as if I had walked through a shower. This had been caused by a combination of hard work in a confined space, the very high temperature in the corridors and passageways and the high pressure hose spraying water for a total of one and a half hours. I also was wearing the fire boots which had been given to me during the fire fighting. Tucked down the side of one of the fire boots was a heavy duty torch. What a sight I must have looked as I searched the ship for Noreen.

During my search, many of the passengers approached me and asked if the ship would have to be evacuated. I had been already calculating that during the ninety minutes that I had been involved, my hose had been discharging 100 gallons every minute. That means that I had been responsible for pumping about 9000 gallons of water into the ship.

I knew that by now there were three other fire fighting teams, pumping on board the same amount of water. My rough total was 36,000 gallons of water and the fire was still being fought, with hundreds of gallons every minute, still being pumped from the sea onto the fire.

My answer to the many very worried passengers who spoke to me regarding the ship being evacuated was, "A fifty-fifty chance." Little did I know that at 7am, the captain was forced to give the order, Flood the Double Bottom Tanks. This action was necessary to counteract the risk of liquid movement due to the fire fighting. Not only did we have the fire out of control but there was a possibility of the ship capsizing, due to the fire fighting water sloshing around.

As I continued my search for Noreen, I noted that all the ship's life boats had been slung-out, ready for boarding. Also all the passengers were wearing lifejackets.

At this time in the morning, dawn was breaking and I could make out a number of ships on the horizon. They were all coming to our assistance. I counted twelve in all.

It was hard to believe that I was in this situation. Noreen was missing. Was she alive? The ship was burning out of control, rescue vessels were on the horizon and I could hear the sound of helicopters overhead. Looking up, I counted four helicopters and higher in the sky, circling the *Tor Scandinavia*, was a Nimrod plane. This was one almighty rescue operation.

During all my years fighting fires, I had been involved in many major incidents, but this – being on board a burning ship – was my worst experience.

I searched and searched for my wife but I could not find her. I became more and more concerned. I went to the bridge where there were about five of the crew, including the captain. I asked if there had been any casualties. No-one replied. Knowing that deck 5 forward section had not been evacuated, I feared the worst. Still nobody spoke.

I said, "My wife is missing and I cannot find her." The reply received was, "I hope you find her." That was that. How despondent I felt, after all the help I had given, they seemed to show no concern. As I walked slowly out of the bridge to recommence my search, the captain said, "I will send some one to look for her." But he never asked me for a description or even my wife's name.

As I stepped onto the open deck I turned and looked back into the bridge. Nobody was looking at me, nobody bothered to help. I feared the worst. I knew that there had to be casualties. The question was, how many?

I thoroughly searched all the outside decks and the inside corridors. Because I was covered in grime and dirt from the fire, nobody stopped me from entering any part of the ship. I was still wearing the fire boots with the torch tucked down my right boot. This obviously was the reason that I was never once questioned or stopped, even although the captain had posted members of his crew at every stairway, to ensure no passenger was allowed below deck. I searched every part of the ship, every deck, even the badly smoke-damaged corridors. In the lounge I found my two friends Alice and Ron but they had not seen Noreen since leaving our cabin. I continued searching and on returning to the lounge Noreen was there. What a relief! I was never so thankful in all of my life.

Now that we were all together, I said that I was returning to our cabin. Our friends said that there had been an announcement that no one was allowed down to their cabins. I told them that I had to change out of my wet clothing and anyway the crew were allowing me to go where I pleased. The three of them then asked me to retrieve some of their personal belongings, such as toiletries.

As I made my way down I could not help noticing the difference in the passageways and corridors. Gone were the bright clean walls and carpets. Everything was covered in smoky grime – a scene that I had witnessed too often. Cabin doors were lying open due to a hasty rush to safety. The scene was exactly the same as many a large hotel fire – dark, smoky and the prolonged pungent smell of cables having been burnt through.

As I made my way along deck 5, I met the crew from the German destroyer *Hamburg* and I could not fail to observe how well-trained and professional they were as they went about their duties. When I reached cabin 5023, the two passengers who had died were being carried out of their cabin by the *Hamburg* fire fighters. They were husband and wife, Gunilla and Lars E Larsson from Karlstad, Sweden. They had been on vacation. Both were now in body bags.

As the eight young Germans passed me, four carrying each bag, there was an air of dignity in the fire-damaged corridor as these young men conducted their duties in a solemn manner. I stepped aside to allow them to pass then continued on my way.

When I reached our cabin 5310, what a shambles! It was completely smoke logged and the cabin floor was filled with water. The scene inside the cabin was one of complete devastation – all the bags and shoes that had been neatly stored were all under twelve inches of dirty water, completely ruined. The cabin was changed beyond recognition – bedding, clothes, precious treasures, all lost to heat, smoke and water damage.

As far as the heat and smoke damage was concerned, I knew that the four of us who had shared this cabin, would have stood absolutely no chance of survival. As I changed into dry clothing my feet were sloshing in the water, but my thoughts were how grateful and how very lucky we were, that one of our friends, on hearing a strange noise, went to investigate and on returning wakened Noreen. What she heard was the fire doors banging closed. Thank goodness our friend, Alice is a very light sleeper.

5

WOULD YOU LIKE
A BANANA?

I wakened and watched as my friend, Alice left the cabin,
(writes Noreen Steele). She opened the door quietly and
stepped out, wearing her nightdress. I presumed that she
had left to smoke a cigarette, as she would not have smoked
in the shared cabin. She returned almost immediately and
whispered to me, "the ship is on fire." I did not believe
her but she told me to follow.

To humour her, or so I thought, I climbed down from
my top bunk and we went out into the corridor. On turning
left, our way was barred by a metal door. Alice asked, "was
that there when we went to bed?" My reply was no, and
at that, I felt the stirring of fear in my stomach.

Together we hauled the door open, to reveal a corridor
full of smoke. Alice, hand on hip, said, "See!" I replied,
"Oh no, this cannot be happening."

It was very quiet. No one was to be seen and no alarm
bells were ringing. We hurried back to our cabin to waken
our husbands and John immediately ran towards the fire,
shouting to us, "Waken the people and get them out."

Although we wanted to run away, we could not go
and leave people sleeping in their cabins, unaware that

the ship was on fire and the smoke was creeping along the corridor towards them. Not taking time to dress, I slipped on my body warmer, which was hanging by the door. I then started alerting the passengers by banging on their cabin doors and telling them they had to get out on deck as the ship was on fire.

When I knocked on a cabin door, I waited until it was opened and the occupants were aware of the situation, before I moved onto the next cabin. The shock on people's faces has stuck in my mind. No one had to be told twice. They all reacted very quickly, without panic. Some asked which way to go. But as I did not know, I just kept banging on doors and alerting people.

I met up with John and told him that we should get up to the open deck, but he replied, "You cannot leave people to die." I kept moving along the smoke-filled corridor, thinking, is there no end to the number of doors?

Finally I could go no further – a metal door blocked my way. I was trapped, trapped in the smoke-filled corridor. So this is how it all ends? I have had it, I thought. Frozen with fear, I just stood and imagined my body being found. They would not even know who I was.

Suddenly from behind me, I heard a man shout, "Come now this way." I turned and he was beckoning to me. I ran towards him and recognised him to be one of the musical group because I had seen them earlier, wearing identical blue and green tracksuits.

I ran past him and he called out, "No, this way," pointing to a corridor across the ship. A metal door was opened onto a staircase leading up. I climbed as fast as I could up and up, till I reached the boat deck and the relative safety of the fresh air.

In the darkness on deck, all was quiet. No panic, no noise. The crew had swung the lifeboats out preparing them for use and everyone was wearing lifejackets. The lids of the lockers containing the lifejackets were raised.

"Better take one," I thought, although I did not know how to put it on.

There had been no emergency drill or instructions given and indeed only an impression on our cabin door where supposedly an instruction notice had once been. I was on deck 7 portside near the bridge with only a few other people, the stragglers to reach safety. The majority of the passengers I now know were congregated at the stern in the relative comfort of the lounges. It was now impossible to join them because of the thick, black smoke billowing midship across the deck. It was 5.10am and the ship had come to a standstill.

Fortunately the weather was kind to us. It was dry and not too cold. A woman, whom I took to be a crew member, approached me and said, "Raise your arms," as she took my lifejacket from me. She placed it over my head and pulled the straps very tightly to secure it.

Things must be very serious I thought, but what will I do now? Where is my husband? Where are my friends? Are they still alive?

As I stood quietly I became aware of girls' voices calling for help. They seemed to be down at the bow of the ship but I could not see them in the darkness. A woman beside me answered, "Come up here."

I thought, how stupid! because they would have to go back in where the fire was to come up the staircase. But I didn't voice an opinion. I did not feel as if I were part of all the drama around me – more like an onlooker viewing a film.

The smoke began drifting down on to us making it difficult to breathe. I hung over the side trying to get fresh air. The same woman's voice now shouted, "Follow me, let's get away from the smoke." We were led in single file up a short staircase leading to the bridge. On entering the bridge I was surprised to notice no one there. We hurried through to the exit at the opposite side. After descending another short staircase we were now on the starboard side.

There was still no great number of people standing around. No one was speaking English and I stood alone, apart from the rest, just watching. An elderly lady was carried down from the bridge and sat on a chair. She was having great difficulty breathing. A young Dutch child was crying because she wanted her nappy changed. Her parents looked very scared and clung together. Another lady began creating a fuss because she had no shoes and there was broken glass lying around. A cabin window was duly smashed with a chair and a young lad shoved inside to find some protection for this lady's feet. I was thankful to see him hauled out again as he could have lost his life because of this foolish action.

We were ushered aside as crew members unrolled a fire hose along the deck. I looked at this hose and thought it was empty. I stepped forward and stamped on it and my suspicions were confirmed. There was no water running through the hose. At intervals during the next two hours I stood on the hose never to feel water.

I tried to decide what to do for the best – to go into a lifeboat in the middle of the North Sea in the darkness or stay with the ship and hope to meet up with my husband if he ever managed to get back up.

Would the ship explode if the fire reached the car deck? It might even capsize. What did fate have in store? Would I live to see my grandchild due to be born after Christmas? If I had to get into a lifeboat it would be sensible to be with English-speaking people.

With this in mind I wandered slowly along the deck till I heard English voices. On joining their company a lady said, "Isn't this exciting?" I replied, "Not if your husband is down fighting the fire and you can't find your friends."

I did not feel inclined to join this jolly bunch.

By now pin pricks of light were seen approaching and this offered a small degree of comfort, knowing that other ships were coming to our assistance. As time passed more lights became visible in the surrounding darkness. When daylight finally dawned the smoke was diminishing and I decided to try to make my way to the stern of the ship and possibly find my husband. The deck was littered with various obstacles but I resolutely clambered over them to get past.

I had been confined by the smoke for more than two hours and was anxious to do something constructive now. I was quite taken aback by the scene I came upon. People were scattered around wrapped in blankets, all wearing bright orange lifejackets. Some were sitting in sun loungers, others lying on the deck. I was reminded of a war zone I had seen on television. I made my way through the crowd peering at faces, but I failed to recognize anyone. The loss of my contact lenses did not help matters as I am very short-sighted.

Finding a toilet seemed high on my priority list now and I entered the lounge area to look for one. The lounge was full of people standing around or sitting at tables or on soft seats. They all seemed to be talking. An aura of excitement filled the air.

As I made my way towards some signs on the wall hoping to read, Ladies, I became aware of my name being called. "Noreen, Noreen you're safe!" I turned to see Ron hurrying towards me with arms outstretched. Alice was also there saying, "John's safe. He is looking for you."

We three held on to each other and tried to hug, but our bulky lifejackets made it difficult. With the relief of being together came the realization of how funny we looked dressed only in our pyjamas. I was glad I was wearing nice new pink ones.

Just then a crew member stepped forward and spoke the words I will never forget, "Would you like a banana?" We declined her kind offer and were then asked, "Would you like a piece of chicken? It is still frozen but it will soon thaw out." It seemed sensible at the time and didn't strike us as funny till later.

I suddenly found myself being embraced by a complete stranger, who was calling to her friend, "That's the Scots voice that saved us." This was to happen on more than a few occasions that day as people heard the four Scots speaking.

John then appeared, still wearing pyjamas but now had fireman's boots with a torch tucked into one. He was soaked through and smelled of smoke. I was reminded of his days with the fire brigade.

Instead of a fond reunion he said, "Where on earth have you been? No-one could find you. Did you go back down? Just where were you?" He told us to stay together here, that the fire was still burning and that people had died. John thought he would try to get back to our cabin for some dry clothes for himself. He asked, "I'll bring you something back each – what do you want?" I asked for my tracksuit, Alice wanted her handbag and Ron a pair of socks.

As John stood up I noticed the chair he had been sitting on was now soaked from his dripping wet pyjamas. Through the window I could see another much smaller boat tied alongside us. I was startled to see the name of it *Poisidon*.

We could hear helicopters overhead and I moved out onto the open deck to watch. It was an awesome sight to see the medics being lowered on to the deck, dangling at the end of a rope. The noise was deafening and the strong down draught from the blades all but swept the people on deck away.

As I sheltered behind an iron staircase I saw all the blankets blowing about while the passengers desperately tried to hold on to them. In different circumstances it would have been a comical sight. The medics moved quickly and efficiently around giving assistance where required. The badly injured were hoisted up on stretchers into the helicopters to be whisked away to hospital. It must have been terrifying for them. I was wearing only one shoe now as I had given one to Alice, who had cut her feet on broken glass. I reckoned one each to be better than none.

John returned looking a bit better with the soot washed away and wearing a dry change of clothes. I was glad to have a tracksuit and pulled it on over my pyjamas. Other people were wearing an odd assortment of clothes. Some in dressing gowns and slippers, some walking around like ancient Roman citizens with only bedsheets draped around themselves. Still others were perfectly dressed and even carried suitcases. We were instructed to remain wearing our lifejackets. A cup of tea would have been most welcome but it wasn't possible for hot drinks to be provided.

However an abundance of free beer was readily available. This helped somewhat to relax the weary passengers – the four of us sat round a table and partook of a few beers. The staff busied themselves laying out huge buffet tables with a variety of cold food. An announcement asked that the food was not to be touched till the preparations were complete. A few grabbed a handful, although there was a plentiful supply.

A short time later, one of the officers came and shook John's hand, saying he was glad John was aboard and that he did not know what he would have done without his help. He said that a fire was the last thing he ever expected aboard his ship. He introduced himself as Pelle Orsted, Chief Officer. He then gave John his business card.

There was still a buzz of activity round us, with many other ships encircling the *Tor Scandinavia*. There were helicopters and a Nimrod plane, which was said to be in charge of the rescue operation. We were to turn back and head for Denmark. This we did and proceeded slowly under escort. It was a relief when we were finally allowed to take our lifejackets off, though the bruises they caused, lasted for many days.

I now wanted to go back down to deck 5, where it had all started. I always like to get to the bottom of things. I had to see where the fire had started and what damage it had done. I wanted to see where I had been trapped, where I thought I was going to die. I just had to go and look, to see it all for myself. I was determined no one would stop me.

John led the way. There were two of the crew posted at the top of the stairs, but as John was still wearing fire boots and carrying the torch, they let us pass.

We made our way down to deck 5. On reaching it, I had to pull my trousers up to my knees, as the deck was under about 12 inches of black sooty water. All the cabin doors were lying open, showing the obvious signs of the hasty evacuation. As we moved along the corridor, the dirty water sloshed about in waves. We came across a fire hose, lying on the floor, with water still pouring from it. I felt a pang of fear, thinking that the ship might capsize with all the water that had been pumped into her and still was all these hours later.

Our cabin, number 5310, resembled the scene from a disaster. Had we really been sleeping peacefully here, the previous night? It was now waterlogged with various items such as socks and shoes floating around. Little soot-covered tubs of yogurt had escaped from the picnic hamper and had stayed huddled together, bobbing up and down in the water, like a flock of sea birds.

46

Next, John took me to what had been the seat of the fire, a linen store. Nothing remained except blackened twisted metal frames, which I presumed to be linen trolleys. Everything else was burned completely away. The fire had burned through to the adjoining cabin and even the bed was scorched black. I felt sick with fear for the passengers who had occupied this cabin. Surely no-one could have survived this nightmare. Why did the ship not have a sprinkler system? It would have given us all a chance to escape, time to find our way out of this maze of corridors.

I was getting angry now. Why no sprinklers, why no alarm, why no crew to help us, why close the fire doors and shut us in with the fire? Questions would have to be answered.

I tried to figure out where I had been trapped and thinking that I was going to die, but I did not know where I had been. The smell of the smoke became nauseating – time to head back up to the fresh air.

We came across the hose that had been gushing water on the way down. It was turned off now and two young crew members were trying to separate the two lengths of hose, but couldn't. John showed them how. One of them said to John, that he had seen him fighting the fire at six o'clock that morning.

We returned to the lounge and joined our friends again, sitting at the table. Everyone was given insurance forms to fill out. This kept us all occupied, trying to think what had been left behind and ruined in our cabins. Luckily we had only taken overnight bags with us, having left our suitcases in the car. I was sorry my camera had been ruined as I would like to have taken snaps. Also my contact lenses were lost.

We slowly progressed towards Esbjerg, with time now to think about our situation. I realized that although we were underway again, we were sailing in the opposite direction, away from home. Families were expecting us and would not know where we were. We had no means of getting in touch and we did not know when we would return home.

I passed the day, just watching people. The passengers were mostly in little groups, engaged in animated conversation, swopping stories about their experiences. We were allowed back to our cabins to retrieve what belongings we could salvage. Very many people were too afraid to venture below decks. Fellow passengers, Brian and Jean Hindle returned with a few things but Brian's camera was ruined. When Jean opened her vanity case a vast amount of water came pouring out of it. It was good to meet up with the Hindles again as we had shared a bottle of wine earlier and had enjoyed their company. Brian suggested we exchange addresses and we did.

As we neared Esjberg, an announcement was made over the loudspeaker system. I could not believe what I was hearing. It was announced that the fire had been started deliberately in the linen store. This could be confirmed as traces of inflammable liquid had been found on the linen. The announcement went on, that any one of the passengers could have been responsible for this.

My immediate reaction was to shout, "That is not true." I felt outrage. I had seen the linen cupboard with my own eyes. There was no linen left to examine. "I am going to tell him a thing or two," I stated. John put a restraining hand on my arm, saying, "Not now, you are too angry."

I was furious, for them to say that any one of the passengers could have been responsible, not any one on board. Did this place us under suspicion but not the crew? I still held the belief that the fire had been caused by a carelessly discarded cigarette.

6

BACK TO DRY LAND

It was still daylight as the *Tor Scandinavia* limped into the harbour at Esjberg. The lifeboats were still dangling over the side. How we wished it was Harwich. We had a fine vantage point at the bow of the ship, high up on deck 7.

There seemed to be a lot of activity on the dockside awaiting our arrival. Another ship similar to ours was already berthed and as we manoeuvred in beside her, we saw it was the *Dana Anglia*.

The damage to our ship was not very obvious as it was all below deck. Later we were to learn that it was to cost £5million to rectify the fire, smoke and water damage to make the *Tor Scandinavia* seaworthy again.

We now knew that two passengers had lost their lives. In our minds we could still see the burned-out cabin they had they been trapped in. They would have stood no chance at all. Little did we know that the cabin was to haunt Noreen's dreams for many, many long months.

Since during the previous twenty four hours, we had been to hell and back, we anxiously waited to be allowed to leave the ship. At last the moment had come. After gathering together our few belongings we set off. Why we carried with us a polythene bag containing John's soaking wet, smoke-soiled pyjamas, we'll never know!

An announcement was made that we would be boarding the *Dana Anglia* to sail home. We thought the foot passengers were fortunate not to have to go down through the ship to get off. They made their exit via the gangways. The four of us decided to stay together and head down to our car and we joined the queue waiting to get to the vehicle deck.

The bedraggled bunch of passengers made their way reluctantly down to the car deck to drive their vehicles off the ship onto the quay at Esjberg. It was very frightening for some, to descend down through the vessel, now soot-covered and blackened by the recently extinguished fire. The thought of finally getting off the badly damaged *Tor Scandinavia* and leaving the nightmare behind, gave them the courage to keep descending the seemingly endless flights of stairs. The families kept close together and hurriedly scrambled into their cars with relief.

Unfortunately, to add to their misery, the powers that be decided to interview each occupant of every car, before allowing them to drive off the ship. This was too much for some to cope with and many collapsed in tears, while others shouted their annoyance.

"Just let us off," was the plea. Meanwhile, the exhaust fumes created by the over anxious drivers built up around them, reminiscent of the smoke from the fire they had earlier escaped from.

Finally after being allowed to drive off and directed into parking bays, the passengers were now faced with an array of news reporters and camera men, all wanting details of their ordeal aboard the *Tor Scandinavia*. Meanwhile a fleet of ambulances ferried the injured to hospital.

After twenty four hours at sea, what was to happen to us next was uppermost in most people's minds. After all this time we had only reached Denmark. The North

Sea would still have to be crossed to reach home.

All passengers were now faced with an option requiring an immediate decision – either drive straight onto the *Dana Anglia* and sail once more into the darkness, for a long overnight journey home, or stay locally before tackling the trip home the following morning. Either way, the crossing had to be made, sooner or later. Some felt if they did not continue with their journey now, they never would. Some couples disagreed about what to do for the best. Mostly the women wanted home as soon as possible, to get it all behind them. Little did they know the ordeal and chaos awaiting them on the *Dana Anglia*.

We decided to board the *Dana Anglia* as we wanted home as soon as possible. After the car was guided into the lane for embarkation, we left the car and mingled with other people on the quayside. Martin Frizzell from ITN news starting filming and interviewing John. This was seen at home on the 7am news by our family, who had already decided among themselves that if the ship was on fire, their dad would run to the fire and not away from it.

We were asked if we would travel to London, on ITN's private plane, to appear on breakfast television and give a first hand account of our experiences. We agreed to this and our friends said they would drive the car onto the ship and meet us at Harwich. As we waited for the arrangements the cars were driven onboard.

Feeling insecure about the whole night's events, Noreen suddenly changed her mind about going to London for the TV show. "After what we've been through, we should all stay together," she said. John agreed and Noreen ran on ahead, panicking in case the *Dana Anglia* would leave without us, as the gangway had been removed, ready for sailing. She ran onto the car ramp and stood there till John came along. She reckoned that the ramp couldn't be raised while she was standing on it.

51

As we walked onto the ship, we were asked for our tickets. Our reply was, "we are from the burning ship," and the crewman motioned us to proceed, saying that we were to report to the purser's office to be allocated cabins.

We made our way up through the ship, to look for our friends and find out what arrangements had been made for us. On reaching the deck, where the purser's office was situated, we were shocked to come upon a seething mass of people, crowding and pushing towards the purser's office window.

Mixed together with the troubled passengers from the *Tor Scandinavia* were the passengers who were already booked on the *Dana Anglia* and were going on holiday. They had been told to get their tickets for the cinema from the purser's office. Some of them were showing their annoyance at these people who had delayed their voyage and were now holding up the queue for the cinema tickets.

The people from the burning ship should be kept separate, was the repeated complaint. Alas, no common sense was brought into the situation and the overwrought people were left to join the jostling throng. Could the *Tor Scandinavia* passengers not have been seated in the lounge, with a welcome cup of tea and a few words of comfort, then allocated cabins?

Some opted to spend the journey on deck after being issued with cabins in the bowels of the ship.

Many cabins were below the car deck. No allowance was made for the trauma they had come through – just a take-it-or-leave-it attitude. Food vouchers were given out, to be used the following day, but nothing for that evening. No provision was made to allow messages to be sent home to inform the anxiously waiting friends and relatives as to what was happening.

The media had announced that there had been two fatalities, but no names had been given. Passengers from the burning ship were clambering to use the ship-to-shore telephone, but once the *Dana Anglia* departed, the telephone could no longer be used. This caused more than a few tears and despair among the long-suffering passengers.

John hurriedly made his way to the ship's radio room. He explained, "I am from the burning ship. I helped to put out the fire and I want to phone home. I fought the fire with this man." (showing Pelle Orsted's card) The use of the phone was made freely available to him and Ron, who had followed him to the radio room.

At least, now our families knew we were safe.

Thankfully our cabin was not below the car deck and we went for a wash and tidy up. We tried to have a sleep but found it impossible to stay in the cabin. We spent the remainder of the voyage sitting around the lounges.

The passengers from the burning ship (as they became known) were easily picked out by their restless behaviour and nervous manner.

At last, the night was over. People began to pull their wits together and make the best of things. A visit to the duty free shop would pass the time. The duty free shop had a special offer of table wines in engraved carafes. Thoughts of that being a good souvenir were soon dashed, as the shop staff insisted on seeing our boarding passes for the *Tor Scandinavia* before allowing us to purchase this offer.

When fleeing for one's life from a fire, salvaging a boarding pass is not a priority, but try telling that to Scandinavian Seaways staff. We were angry and insisted on speaking to the purser about the stupidity of this. He allowed us purchase the wine.

John was called over the tannoy, to go to the radio room to receive a telephone call from Ross Wilson of the *Daily Record* newspaper in Glasgow. John had been shown on early morning television and the paper wanted a first hand account of all that had been happening. John was quite willing to answer all of their questions. He also agreed to be interviewed on reaching Harwich.

What a feeling of relief to be driven off that ship at Harwich. On the dockside we spotted a chap holding a placard aloft with JOHN STEELE written on it. We pulled in to speak to him and discovered that he was the news reporter. After that, it was homeward bound.

WITNESS ACCOUNT
Brian and Jean Hindle from Bury

We were wakened, from our sleep, by loud shouting in the corridor outside our cabin. I told Brian (my husband) to go back to sleep as it was nothing to do with us but he got out of bed and opened the door.

He was shocked to see the corridor full of smoke and was told that the ship was on fire. As if on auto pilot we quickly dressed. Brian being worried about my asthma, he wet a towel and draped it around my head before we left the cabin. We made our way along the passageway through the smoke but our progress was halted by a closed fire door. Fortunately we were shown an exit to flights of stairs leading up onto an upper deck.

When we came out onto the open deck we saw many people just standing crying and we realised we were walking over broken glass. When I saw the lifeboats hanging over the ship's side I thought "Oh my God, this is for real. It is not just a bad dream."

Brian reassured me that it was alright – it was only procedure in an emergency. A member of the crew was helping people with their lifejackets and she said it was very serious. Most of the passengers around us were wearing their night clothes. One lady was wearing a black dress and white shoes. I remembered seeing her dancing the previous evening and I thought, "how odd!" Now here she was dressed the same but with the addition of a bright orange lifejacket and carrying a white plastic bag probably containing a few hastily grabbed belongings.

Later a member of the crew came round dispensing coffee in half pint glasses and biscuits from a large tin. He said chicken legs and bread rolls would be served in one of the lounges.

We were shocked to see this once beautiful lounge/dining room now a shambles and covered in soot. We had dined there earlier and had been entertained by a man playing the grand piano. He had looked very elegant in his white jacket with a red carnation in his lapel.

We watched the sun rising above the calm sea. It was a beautiful morning. A speedboat came alongside and unloaded oxygen bottles, up the side of our ship, to a crew member. More and more ships gathered around us. I counted fourteen in all. One ship stayed alongside and acted as a barge for loading and unloading bottles of oxygen for the people fighting the fire.

Brian said, "Look at the name. It is called *Poseidon.* I hope that is not an omen." A German navy ship was standing off and a large boat from it was making its way towards us. The navy personnel on board it looked immaculately dressed in grey outfits with one or two in silver fire fighting kit. They were sitting very erect and looked determined to put out the fire which was still burning. We found some duvet quilts and settled ourselves on deckchairs to try to sleep but Brian was very restless. He found a doctor who was attending to people suffering from smoke inhalation and asked him what he should do if I suffered an asthma attack. He told him not to worry as they had medication if I needed it.

Helicopters came to the ship, airlifted the injured and took them to hospital 100 miles away in Esbjerg. It was quite frightening to watch the injured being winched from the ship and dangling in mid-air, then helped aboard the hovering helicopter.

My feet were very cold, as in my haste to reach the open deck I had slipped on a pair of sandals. For some reason, I had put a pair of Brian's socks in my pocket. They were pale blue and yellow, my sandals were red, but what the heck!

In the afternoon, we were allowed to return to our cabins. To do so, we had to wade through a foot or so of water. On entering our cabin we saw a sweater floating about. A friend of Brian's had given the sweater to him as a birthday present. It was weird, as if it had a life of it's own, waving its arms around as if it was dancing.

That is when I cried, thinking that it could have been Brian floating about. On leaving the cabin, we passed other passengers collecting their belongings and one teenager threw down his canvas holdall, declaring, "I am not taking that, it is ruined."

Later on, the captain came into the lounge and informed us that the ship was turning around and sailing to Esjberg in Denmark, where we would disembark and board another ship which would take us to Harwich.

During the voyage to Esjberg, some members of the crew handed out claim forms for us to complete. I really think it was to give us something to do, to pass the time.

As we approached the port of Esjberg we were instructed to proceed to the car deck. We went down to our car with what remained of our luggage. Sitting in the car we could smell the smoke, even inside the car. It was such a relief when the bow doors of the ship opened and we were allowed to drive onto the dock side.

When we drove on board the *Dan Anglia*, our roles reversed. I felt that Brian had done his bit, to get us on to a safe ship and now it was my turn to organise things, such as, we were in need of a meal, a drink and a well earned rest. Brian was suddenly exhausted and was content to be guided by myself. I think as a couple, it was our way of coping with the stress and it worked very well for us.

By now, we had been up for over twelve hours, we were told to wait in a queue and we would be allocated a cabin and given a meal voucher. This seemed to take ages and when we reached the front of the queue we discovered that it was also for the passengers of the *Dan Anglia* wishing to purchase tickets for the cinema. By now, we were all at the end of our tether.

In the dining room there was a couple sitting next to us. The lady was unsure what to order and the man sitting with her shouted that she should pull herself together and order something. When he saw me looking at him he smiled sweetly and said, "don't mind us", but I did mind, very much.

Thinking about the incident later, I mentioned it to Brian and he said perhaps it was his way of dealing with the situation.

Once in our cabin we felt that we wanted to shut the whole world out, feeling that it was a terrible place out there, with nothing but noise and screaming children. Of course they had no idea of the ordeal we had come through. We had been in a terrible fire on board a ship in the middle of the North Sea and survived.

Looking back, it could have been handled so much better. People were wandering in a daze and I felt that we were treated as an inconvenience to the crew and passengers of the *Dan Anglia*. There had been no apology or any contact from the shipping company.

When we tried to claim from our own holiday insurance company because of the delay, they wrote back to say that no claim was possible as the insurance only covered delayed departure and the *Tor Scandinavia* had sailed on time.

It has taken a long time to go back on board ferries since that terrible incident in our lives. We started with a short trip to the Isle of Wight. It was terrible at first but you have to carry on or you will not go anywhere.

7

THE AFTERMATH

On returning home, I was quite perturbed about many safety aspects in the experience we had (writes John Steele). When I was involved with the passenger evacuation and the fire fighting, there seemed to me to be some serious shortcomings.

After discussing the full events including the part played by Noreen, Alice, Ron and other passengers, I compiled a list of items that I considered needed serious consideration.

I then made an appointment with my Member of Parliament for North Cunningham, in the West of Scotland. Brian Wilson MP is the Opposition spokesman for Transport.

Brian Wilson sent the list to the Danish Embassy in London and they forwarded a copy to the Danish Maritime Authority in Copenhagen. The list included:

1 On none of the three voyages we made did any emergency drill take place;
2 No alarm sounded;
3 There were no emergency lights;
4 No sprinkler system operated;
5 Numerous emergency buttons were activated with no response;

6 No verbal emergency intructions were given on any of
   our three voyages
7 There was no cabin search for survivors during the initial
   fire fighting operation;
8 The ship was unable to transmit SOS on a main
   frequency;
9 Fire hose length was too short;
10 Only small air bottles were supplied with 30 minutes
   supply only (onshore fire brigades use air bottles that
   last one hour);
11 There was no spanner available to change air bottles;
12 The ship's supply of air bottles was used up and fire
   fighting ceased until another ship arrived with a fresh
   supply;
13 There was no back-up team with breathing apparatus
   to assist the fire-fighters;
14 A passenger (John Steele) was the first person to go
   into the fire wearing breathing apparatus;
15 Chief engineer was back-up to John Steele – a passenger
   in pyjamas and bare feet led the firefighting team;
16 Information to passengers during the emergency was
   inadequate;
17 The passenger list was not checked until eight hours
   after the start of the fire;
18 The linen room where the fire started had been left open;
19 The fire exit door from deck 5 had a sign on it saying
   Crew Only.

The reply from the ship's owners, DFDS, made in a letter,
answered these questions point by point as follows.
1 Emergency ship drills would cause inconvenience to the
   passengers.
2 The alarm was sounded but it appeared later that some
   of the emergency cables had been burned by the fire.

3 The ship was fitted with emergency lights all over. These lights were placed in the ceilings of the corridors and cabins, but due to the heavy smoke the light from these was significantly reduced.

4 The ship is built from noncombustible material and consequently no sprinkler system is installed. This is in accordance with SOLAS regulations.

5 The emergency buttons which were activated did give a response in the bridge, where they indicated fire alarm in various areas of the ship. These alarms created some uncertainty as to the extent of the fire.

6 Emergency instructions will be given in all our ships as a result of this incident.

7 The evacuation teams did carry out a cabin search for survivors very soon after the alarm sounded. This operation was much more time-consuming than expected. Following this incident the evacuation teams have been reorganised with more crew members involved in the evacuation of the passengers, in order to reduce the time of evacuation.

8 The captain decided to use the VHF radio installed in the bridge and this turned out to be sufficient.

9 Each hose has a standard length and it is possible to connect together as many hoses as is required.

10 This is the only type of approved breathing apparatus bottle allowed on board ships.

11 The spanner should have been available and of course all bottles were changed during firefighting operations.

12 Although the ship was supplied with more than double the number required she ran out of a supply of air bottles from her own stock. Sufficient supply was available from other ships.

13 The firefighters were made up two persons to a team, with one backing up the other.

14 The assistance of John Steele was highly appreciated but the ship's firefighters would have attacked the fire even if John Steele had not been on board.

15 John Steele gave the impression of being a competent firefighter, which he certainly was and by accepting John Steele's offer, the chief officer's judgement was that he and John Steele formed the most effective firefighting team.

16 The information from the loudspeakers was hampered by the burnt-out cables. These same speakers are used for information purposes and fire alarm purposes.

17 The passenger check was not conducted until the situation had calmed down, all cabins had been searched and the ship management knew for certain that no passengers were in the cabins. The greatest advantage of the passenger check is of course to account for persons still missing in the very early phase of the incident. Later on it does not matter whether the passenger check is carried out two, four or eight hours after an incident.

18 The linen room was not open but some containers holding linen had been stored in the hall area before they could be properly stored in the linen room. This procedure has changed and no linen will be stored in any public area.

19 All emergency doors are marked Emergency Exit, but of course it was also possible to get away from the fire area through the Crew Section.

In a letter to John Steele dated 28 March 1990, DFDS, being very responsible shipping owners, stated that they had implemented certain improvements:

The *Tor Scandinavia* complied fully with Danish and international regulations. However as a result of the fire we found it prudent and logical to introduce improvements as is usually done after disasters. These improvements were:

1 Patrols increased from one per hour to two per hour;
2 A compressor installed with the capacity to refill all the ship's breathing apparatus bottles;
3 Smoke detectors fitted in all alleyways and public areas in addition to the internationally required heat detectors;
4 Photo-luminescent signs fitted at low level to show escape routes;
5 A new, reorganised evacuation group;
6 Two extra sets of breathing apparatus per deck;
7 Escape apparatus for passengers;
8 New fire alarms with high temperature cables the minimum noise level from the alarm will be 100 decibels and 130 decibels in high noise areas;
9 Cabin search to commence as soon as possible after an incident.

Around this time the International Maritime Organisation held many meetings to discuss fire safety as did the International Chamber of Shipping, as a result of which the above improvements suggested by DFDS were adopted as well as:

The crews of all passenger ships involved in the International Maritime Organisation must wear a uniform or other apparel which will distinguish them from passengers.
Emergency lights to be lowered.
Emergency intructions to be given on all voyages.
Extra firefighting equipment to be available.

These fire safety improvements were implemented as a result of a meeting of the International Maritime Organisation, (Sub Committee on Fire Protection) June 1990. It was recorded at the same meeting that, "The current regulations for the protection against fire and operational fire readiness, do not provide a satisfactory level of safety."

The *Tor Scandinavia*

Tor Scandinavia was launched in November 1975. The management was taken over by the Tor Line one year later.

In December 1981, the ship was purchased by DFDS of Denmark. For the next ten months, she sailed between Felixtowe and Gothenburg.

On October 25th 1982, along came another change of name, this time it was *World Wide Expo* and the ship was transformed into a floating exhibition hall for European manufacturing companies.

On December 10th 1982, the ship departed from Copenhagen, bound for Singapore, via the Suez Canal For the next fourteen months she sailed to Bangkok, Tanjung, Berhala, Singapore, Jakarta, Manila and various other ports, before leaving the Far East, on the February 1, 1983 bound for Copenhagen.

During the exhibition voyage as *World Wide Expo*, the diving ship *Skraep* was re-named *Tor Scandinavia* in order to reserve the name. This allowed *World Wide Expo* to revert back to *Tor Scandinavia* in time for her sailings between Gothenburg -Felixstowe-Amsterdam, which commenced on the March 3, 1983

In late 1979, the ship managed the unusual feat of running aground outside Gothenburg on successive departures—on December 23 when bound for Felixstowe and on December 28 when leaving for Amsterdam. Another stain on her good name took place when she was withdrawn from her Harwich to Gothenburg schedule, due to gearing problems which reduced her speed to 15 knots.

More trouble lay ahead when she entered the dry dock at Kristiansand. On the morning of June 30, 1994, at 0530, she fell off the blocks and ended up with an 11 degree list to starboard. Damage was sustained to the hull, which was holed. However the hole was plugged before the dock was flooded to straighten up the ship.

Time table of events regarding the serious and fatal fire on board the ro-ro passenger ferry *Tor Scandinavia* in the North Sea, 100 miles west of Esjberg, on 25th September 1989.

4am. Chief Officer takes over watch.

4.55am Fire alarm activated on bridge fire alarm panel.

4.56am Captain on the bridge.

5.am Lifeboats made ready for evacuation.

5.40am Captain aware of extent of the fire.

6.30am Ships air bottles, for the firemen wearing breathing apparatus, exhausted.

6.40am Full air bottles taken on board from assisting vessels.

7am ships Double Bottomed Tanks flooded to counteract risk of free liquid movement, due to fire-fighting

7.10am The assisting vessel *Maersh Assister* comes alongside – this ship has a compressor to refill air bottles

7.20am Emergency hospital set up in crew's lounge on deck 9.

7.37am Two fire fighters come on board from assisting ship.

7.50am Amount of water from fire fighting approaching serious levels. Require pumps to bale out the water; firefighters also required from surrounding ships who have come in response to May-day message.

8.30am First injured passenger evacuated by helicopter. 10 fire fighters from German destroyer *Hamburg* led by their Commandant, arrive via three helicopters.

8.45am Fire area very hot. Cabin search reveals two passengers found dead in cabin 5023.

10.35am Fire confirmed to be out. Passenger list confirmation complete.

8

ENQUIRY

On Thursday September 28, 1989, at 10.15am, the maritime court was called to order on board the *Tor Scandinavia* which was lying in the port of Esbjerg. The court assessor, P Hald Anderson was assisted by two other court members, Captain Harald Hansen and Captain Leif Lassan. Marine Superintendent Jann Lund was in attendance on behalf of the ship's owners, DFDS. Assistant Chief Constable Henrik Anderson represented the police.

The maritime court carried out a survey of the badly damaged ship. They also studied a set of drawings of the *Tor Britannia*, an identical sister ship of the *Tor Scandinavia*. The court was then adjourned, to reconvene on Thursday October 5, 1989 at 11am.

When the court was reconvened, Jann Lund had been replaced as the representative for DFDS by Attorney Arne Engel, Technical Director Frede Kristiansen and Naval Architect Flemming G Hansen.

Chief Marine Superintendent Drachmann represented the maritime authority, Copenhagen.

Mr Johanson, there as an expert surveyor, represented Baltica, Copenhagen.

Marine Superintendents Ole Sobye, GS Thomsen and Bent Hau, all represented the maritime authority, Esbjerg.

The court assessor and the two captains were presiding. Once more representing the police was the assistant chief constable. The officials present in the court numbered twelve of which three represented DFDS.

The witnesses called to give evidence during the two day hearing numbered six, the six principal officers from the *Tor Scandinavia* – the captain, chief officer, radio officer, chief engineer, purser and chief purser.

Of the five hundred and thirty nine passengers, not one was called to give evidence. Of the fire fighters from the *Tor Scandinavia* numbering seven crew and one passenger, only one was called to give evidence, the chief officer.

The captain from the German destroyer *Hamburg* who led the team of fire fighters, all highly trained men, was never called. Neither was the captain and crew of the German marine research vessel *Poseidon*, the first ship to render assistance at 06.40. The list of those not called to give evidence goes on – captain and officers of *Maersh Assister* the ship which supplied the badly needed air bottle compressor plant; the two fire fighters from a rescue vessel who came on board to assist in bringing the fire under control; the crew from the four helicopters who airlifted badly injured personnel; the twenty British anaesthetists who had attended a conference in Sweden and were fortunately onboard the *Tor Scandinavia* thus able to render valuable medical assistance to the injured passengers.

The court opened under the official title and object, Civil Case 6b/89 Maritime inquiry concerning the outbreak of fire on 25 September 1989, at 04.55 onboard *Tor Scandinavia* in the foremost staircase shaft on deck 5, during the ship's voyage from Gothenburg to Harwich.

The first witness called was Captain Orvur Thomassen, the ship's captain. The captain reported the following:

At about 04.55, on being wakened by the crew alarm, I got out of bed and quickly dressed. I made my way along the crew corridor in order to reach the bridge. The corridor was filled with dense smoke and I had to bend down and crawl. I passed a fire door which was open. I did not close it as I knew my crew would be making their way behind me to the bridge.

On entering the bridge the chief officer reported to me the action he had taken. I ordered him to alert the passengers and he activated the passenger alarm and the general alarm.

Due to a build-up of dense smoke in the bridge, both of us had to go outside to the starboard wing of the bridge. We remained there for a short time to get fresh air and to ascertain the direction and speed of the wind.

On re-entering the bridge I ordered the course to be altered and set the ship's speed at eight knots, so that the dense smoke would cause the least possible trouble. I then gave orders to close the fire doors throughout the ship and to open the sluice valves. Whilst on the starboard bridge-wing with the chief officer, we heard several windows being broken and looked down to see the head of the radio officer, Kristen Kjaergaard, at one of the broken windows. When he arrived on the bridge I ordered him to send an emergency call for help, as I judged that due to the fire, there could be a danger to the passengers, the crew and the ship. I also instructed him to request immediate fire fighting assistance and fire fighting equipment.

As we were slightly south of the Dan oil field where there would be much shipping, there was a possibility of receiving rapid assistance from other seafarers in that area. We received an immediate reply from the German marine research ship *Poseidon*. They reported that they were 30 nautical miles from us and were coming at full speed to our assistance.

We also received a reply from the drilling

platform *Gorm Charlie*. They reported that they had transmitted an emergency call to the rescue authorities on land, a distance of 100 miles away from us.

Many other vessels acknowledged our Mayday message and had changed course, sailing at full speed, to help us.

Immediately after this, I spoke into the ship's public address system. I spoke in Scandinavian and English, informing the passengers that the ship was on fire and I requested them to make their way to the smoke free areas. I repeated the warning several times. However I do not recall my precise words and I cannot say whether 10 or 15 minutes elapsed between calls to the passengers.

During the next ten minutes, the indicator lights on the fire warning panel were activated, showing that the ship was on fire in several locations in the areas between deck 5 and deck 9. As a result of the number of different lights flashing on the fire panel, I did not know the extent of the fire.

While this was happening, the chief radio officer appeared on the bridge. He told me that he had been wakened by the crew alarm and had gone to the radio room. However the radio room was so full of smoke that he closed the fire dampers and opened one of the windows, which is also an emergency exit, and crawled out on to the deck. He told me that because of the smoke, he could not stay in the radio room. I told him that it was alright as we had managed to transmit a Mayday message on the VHF radio and help was on the way.

I decided that my chief radio officer should be in command of internal communications. However as I looked at him, I realised that he was suffering very badly from severe smoke inhalation and I knew that he was not fit for duty, I therefore told him to go onto the open deck, to the fresh air.

I was in constant contact, via the hand held radios, with all my senior officers. Chief Officer

Pelle Orsted informed me at 5.05am that fire fighting had commenced. It was reported to me that some of my crew had to be lowered over the ship's starboard side, to rescue passengers who were trapped on decks 5, 6 and 7. The crew members in question, crawled along the Jack stays, on the ship's side and smashed the windows of the cabins where the passengers were trapped. These passengers were rescued by climbing up a ladder, strapped to the ship's side.

At 7 am, I ordered that the passengers on the open deck should be issued with blankets and quilts. I then spoke through the public address system, informing the passengers about the situation regarding the fire fighting. At this point, the *Maersk Assister* came along the port side, took all our empty air bottles on board and re-charged them using their compressor.

On being asked on the ship's radio if a doctor was required, I replied yes, as I knew that many of those on board were suffering from severe smoke inhalation. Two Norwegian nurses were lowered from a helicopter and with the assistance of three doctors who had been travelling as passengers, an emergency hospital was set up in the crew's lounge.

It was then reported to me that the fire fighters had extinguished the fire in deck 5 but deck 6 was still on fire. Two fire fighters from nearby ships came onboard to assist my own men and at about the same time I was informed that there were 'free fluid surfaces'. As this could affect the *Tor Scandinavia's* centre of gravity, I requested a bilge pump from a nearby ship.

The first passengers were evacuated by helicopter at 8.30am. At the same time, ten fire fighters came on board from the German destroyer *Hamburg* and they relieved my crew in the fire fighting.

On his own initiative my chief officer searched the cabins on the starboard side of deck 5. He found two passengers in cabin 5023. One of the doctors on board was summoned and after examining the two passengers he announced them to be dead. After checking the booking list and checking the passports found in the cabin, the two fatalities were identified as Gunilla and Lars E Larsson, a married couple from Karlstad, Sweden. They had been on vacation.

At 10.35am the fire was reported to be completely extinguished. At the same time my crew had completed checking the passengers against the passenger list.

This concluded the captain's statement.

Radio Officer Kristen Kjaergaard then appeared as a witness. He stated that he had sailed as a radio operator for nine years and that he had joined the *Tor Scandinavia* in June 1989. In the event of a fire on board it was his duty to report to the officer in command and to operate the VHF transmitter which is in the bridge, also to attend to information being transmitted to the passengers by means of the public address system.

On September 24, he had been on duty until 9pm. At that time, the chief radio officer took over the watch and the witness retired to his cabin. He further stated that at about 5am, he was awakened by someone running around the corridor shouting that there was smoke everywhere. At first he did not respond. However about 30 seconds later the crew fire alarm sounded. He realised that he was trapped in his cabin. He then smashed the armoured glass and crawled through the window.

On reaching the bridge, the captain ordered him to send out Mayday messages. He went over to the chart table, where there is a satellite receiver which registers the ship's position. Due to the smoke which had filled the bridge, he was having great difficulty in breathing. It was also difficult to read the ship's position on the satellite receiver. When he had ascertained the longitude and latitude, he asked the captain to confirm the ship's position and then he commenced transmitting the Mayday messages including the ships call sign which is 'Owen 2'.

Chief Officer Pelle Orsted then appeared as a witness and stated:

> I have been with DFDS since 1979. I joined the *Tor Scandinavia* in April 1987. At 4am on Monday 25 September 1989, I took over the watch, replacing Morten Seles who had been on duty from midnight. At 4.55am a light began flashing on the fire alarm panel, indicating a fire in deck 4 and deck 5. I attempted to reset the alarm panel but this was not possible.
>
> I sent the seaman on duty, Peter Olsen, down to find out what was wrong. I told him to take a portable radio and when he reached deck 8 he transmitted to me that he could smell smoke. At the same time, I could smell smoke in the bridge. I then ran into my cabin, which was beside the bridge, to get my fire fighting equipment. On my return to the bridge I activated the crew alarm and set the engine telegraph at Stop Engine.
>
> I contacted the ship's captain and informed him of the situation. He ordered me to activate the passenger alarm, which I did. He also instructed me to assemble the fire fighters.
>
> When the captain entered the bridge, the smoke was so dense that visibility was down to 50 cm (2 inches). We had to leave the smoke-filled bridge for some fresh air. As I was the officer in charge of the fire fighting team, I made my way down to deck 8 where the fire fighting squad had assembled. After a brief discussion on how best we could tackle the blaze, I issued orders that the fire hoses were to be laid out and by the time this was done, I had

determined that two fire fighters should proceed together along the starboard side of deck 5 and another team, comprising of myself and one other fire fighter, should proceed along the port side of deck 5.

The other fire fighter and I checked our breathing apparatus, made our way to the port side, picked up the hose, opened the door and entered the smoke-filled corridor. As we entered we could feel the intense heat.

Chief Officer Pelle Orsted related in great detail how he and another crew member evacuated passengers and fought the blaze.

However the other crew member was never called to give evidence, or indeed never named. The mysterious crew member was in fact passenger John Steele.

As the chief officer was giving his evidence at the maritime court of enquiry in Denmark, John Steele was giving his statement to Interpol, in Scotland. Both statements matched completely.

As we have already described how John and the chief officer evacuated passengers and fought the raging fire, we pick-up the chief officer's statement from 6.30am, when the ship's supply of air bottles was exhausted and fire fighting ceased.

Chief Officer Pelle Orsted continued:

The chief engineer and the chief purser arrived and we informed the captain of the up-to-date situation. Captain Thomassen suggested that the fire fighters should try and reach the blue hall through the kiosk in deck 5. However before relaying the order I went all the way forward toward the blue hall until I reached the fire door which was very hot. I returned to the red hall and conferred with the chief engineer and the chief purser whether we should do as the captain suggested and we reached the conclusion that it would be too risky as the fire could flare up and spread if we opened the fire door.

At this point, the chief engineer took charge of the fire fighting and I made my way to deck 7 where I ordered some of the crew to lay out more fire fighting hose, to enable us to fight the fire from above. I made my way up to deck 8 where many of the passengers had assembled. As there was a danger of smoke inhalation, I ordered the crew to move the endangered passengers to a smoke free part of the ship.

By this time, some of the vessels that had picked up our Mayday message were arriving and supplying us with more fire fighting equipment. I decided that we should now fight the fire through the starboard corridor and after that was started I realised that the fire was spreading to deck 6 from deck 5.

I met up with the chief purser who had also realised that the fire was in fact spreading to deck 6. Both of us decided that the fire fighters who had boarded *Tor Scandinavia* from other ships should be deployed fighting the fire from deck 6.

At 9am I opened the fire door on the starboard side of Blue Hall and checked the cabins. In cabin number 5023 I found two dead passengers. There was no indication that they had attempted to get out of their cabin

I had not discussed with the chief purser the course of the evacuation.

At this time the court was adjourned until Friday October 6, 1989 at 9am. The maritime court reconvened with all officials present except Mr Johanson who had represented Baltica of Copenhagen

Chief engineer Leif Povelsen appeared as a witness and stated:

I have sailed as chief engineer for eight years, the last two of them on board *Tor Scandinavia*. On being wakened by the crew alarm I reported to the captain on the bridge. He told me that the fire was in the blue stairwell. I ran along the deck and went down into the engine control room. I had no portable radio with me. I ensured that the fire pump was running and that the ventilation system to the passengers' cabins was stopped. After counting the engine room crew I noted that all were present. I ordered a check to be carried out on the engine and I was informed that all was well.

I made my way to the car deck and ensured that there were no problems. I then assisted the stewardesses to evacuate the cabins in deck 2 by leading the passengers to safety. Accompanied by two engineers, we proceeded to deck 5. We knocked on all the cabin doors and led the passengers to safety via the emergency exit, up to deck 8

I reported back to the bridge, to discuss the situation with the captain. We agreed that I should fight the fire from the blue hall. A fire fighter wearing breathing apparatus and I started to fight the fire. However I had no breathing apparatus and as the heat and smoke were so great, I judged that an entire team wearing breathing apparatus was required. Returning to the bridge, I reported my judgement to the captain, also that I had noticed smoke on deck 6.

On my return to deck 5, I met up with the chief purser. Shortly afterwards, Chief Officer Orsted appeared from the smoke-filled corridor with another fire fighter. Both were wearing breathing apparatus. After a discussion with the chief officer, he left me in charge of the fire fighting in deck 5.

The evacuation groups were led by the chief

purser. Whilst in his company I did not ask him if the passenger evacuation was complete.

During all of this time, I noticed that when the public address system was in use, it cancelled the fire alarm and when communication on the public address system was complete, the fire alarm did not restart automatically but had to be reactivated manually.

This concluded the chief engineer's evidence. The ship's purser, Finn Kruger Larsen was called as a witness and he stated that he had sailed on the ship as purser, since May 1987:

My duty in the event of fire was zone leader, in the evacuation group for deck 2. On responding to the crew alarm, I tried to reach deck 2. Due to the smoke I had to go to deck 7, from there to the red hall in deck 5 and continue from there down to deck 2. I cannot say if I heard the passenger alarm.

On arriving at deck 2, I began to unlock the cabin doors and rouse the passengers. A short time later other members of the evacuation group arrived and assisted me. We opened every cabin door and then re-checked. Only then, when I was satisfied that deck 2 had been completely evacuated I went up to deck 5 where I met the chief purser who was in charge of all the evacuation teams. I informed him that deck 2 had been evacuated.

I then went onto the outside deck and asked some of the catering group to investigate in case any of the passengers were missing. On noticing that some of the children on board were wearing adult life jackets, I instructed the catering group to find children's life jackets for them. In conclusion, my task was to evacuate deck 2 and the evacuation group worked well

The sixth and last witness appeared. He was the ship's chief purser Jens Arp-Nielsen:

I have sailed for six years as Purser and Chief Purser on board *Tor Britannia* and *Tor Scandinavia*. In the event of a fire, it is my responsibility to be the leader of the evacuation groups. Every week we hold fire and evacuation drills. During these practices I report to the bridge that all are present. There is no rule that one who reports to the bridge is to wait an acknowledgement. Sometimes the message is repeated from the bridge and sometimes it is not.

My cabin is on deck 8, on the port side. On hearing the crew alarm I immediately got dressed and opened my cabin door. The corridor was full of smoke. I crawled towards the nearest corridor fire door. However on reaching it, I could not open it and I returned to my cabin to consider the situation. I made a new attempt and managed to reach the open deck on the port side. I continued up to the bridge and the captain informed me where the fire had broken out. I continued down to deck 7 where I attempted to enter blue hall. This was impossible because of the smoke. On retracing my steps along deck 7, I attempted to enter into red hall but this was also impossible due to the smoke.

I finally succeeded in reaching deck 5 via the green hall. On my way through the passenger accommodation I did not hear the passenger alarm or the call over the ship's public address system but I did meet some passengers and some crew members.

On reaching my destination, the zone leader and the evacuation group were already there. They had all been given keys to the passengers' cabins and torches. I was obviously the last to arrive. I can give no explanation for this, apart from it depending on the time I was wakened and the fact that as chief purser, I have a separate bedroom. The other members of the group who arrived in the red hall of deck 5 before me, also have cabins on the same deck as I and it made me wonder if all the crew had been wakened by the fire alarm.

In view of this and to make certain, I ordered the information leader to make telephone calls to every one on the telephone crew list. I cannot say if the telephone was working but as I heard nothing to the contrary, I assumed that my order had been carried out.

Within the first five to ten minutes after the fire alarm had sounded, I was receiving reports from the evacuation groups that the passenger cabins on deck 6 and 7 and most of deck 5 had been evacuated. On the basis of the reports which were coming in to me, I became aware that there had been no reports from the crew member who was to arouse the passengers in cabins 5001 to 5023.

I asked some one from either the standby group or the evacuation group to find the crew member in question.

At this time, I became aware that the passengers in the transverse corridor on deck 5 had not been evacuated. I immediately spoke to one of my colleagues who informed me that some steward-esses from the shipping company Stena Line had spent the night in some of the cabins 5001 to 5023. He went on, "the stewardesses were said to have knocked on the doors of cabins 5001 to 5023."

To make certain, three of us, the ship's night watch man, a crew member from the catering group and myself attempted to penetrate into the starboard corridor where the cabins were located. As the person responsible for the evacuation of all the passengers, I wanted to check the entire ship, even although it had been said that the Swedish stewardesses had aroused the passengers in the cabins in question.

The three of us made it to cabin 5001 when we

were forced to give up the search. We then ran over to the port side in order to reach cabins 5002 to 5023. Once more, due to heavy smoke we managed to penetrate only a few metres, then we had to turn back.

I then went to the Red Hall where I met some fire fighters. At this time I had still not received the All Clear from the zone leader on deck 2 and I decided to make my way there with four other members of the evacuation group. I took with me a walkie-talkie radio.

On reaching deck 2 an evacuation team was already alerting the passengers and leading them to safety. I therefore decided to reach deck 4 and when I got there I looked up and could see the flames on deck 5. Some of the ceiling panels and cables started to fall on me. I then made for the car deck and from there I reached deck 5. On listening to the messages on my walkie-talkie radio it became clear that cabins 5001 to 5023 had not been evacuated by the evacuation crew and I reported this information.

I then gave orders to the catering crew to distribute refreshments, blankets and quilts to the passengers. I finally ordered guards at the various stairways to prevent passengers from returning to their cabins. After this I went out to the open deck as I felt ill.

On returning to the information area on deck 5, I saw the chief officer and another fire fighter come out of the smoke-filled corridor, change their air bottles and return into the smoke-filled corridor.

The thought did not strike me that I should have instructed these two fire fighters with breathing apparatus, to check cabins 5001 to 5023. This was because the lifesaving work was in another phase.

Immediately afterwards the chief engineer and I went into the kiosk section. We noted the heavy smoke and the intense heat and I was worried that the stocks might burn. On informing the bridge of this situation, I was instructed to go through the

The Scandinavian Seaways passenger-cargo vessel *Tor Scandinavia* was an imposing sight when viewed from the dockside

On reaching the open deck it was such a relief to breath in fresh air

People were scattered around wrapped in blankets, all wearing bright orange lifejackets — the scene was exactly the same as many a large hotel fire — dark and smoky and the prolonged pungent smell of cables having been burnt through

It was an awesome sight to see the medics being
lowered on to the deck, dangling at the end of a rope

The noise was deafening and the strong down draft
from the blades all but swept the people on deck away

The passenger liner *Prince George* was in dock when smoke was seen. Firefighters eventually stopped pumping water on to the ship and concentrated on saving the dockside. The vessel was allowed to burn itself out

Shipping companies such as Caledonian MacBrayne (above) who participate in evacuation exercises are to be congratulated

A new breed of ship — the HSS1500 coming into service in the summer of 1996 will be capable of carrying 1500 passengers and 375 cars. Even bigger vessels are planned

The Scandinavian Seaways passenger-cargo vessel *Tor Scandinavia* was an imposing sight when viewed from the dockside

On reaching the open deck it was such a relief to breath
in fresh air

People were scattered around wrapped in blankets, all wearing bright orange lifejackets — the scene was exactly the same as many a large hotel fire — dark and smoky and the prolonged pungent smell of cables having been burnt through

It was an awesome sight to see the medics being
lowered on to the deck, dangling at the end of a rope

The noise was deafening and the strong down draft
from the blades all but swept the people on deck away

The passenger liner *Prince George* was in dock when smoke was seen. Firefighters eventually stopped pumping water on to the ship and concentrated on saving the dockside. The vessel was allowed to burn itself out

Shipping companies such as Caledonian MacBrayne
(above) who participate in evacuation exercises are to be
congratulated

A new breed of ship — the HSS1500 coming into service in the summer of 1996 will be capable of carrying 1500 passengers and 375 cars. Even bigger vessels are planned

The Scandinavian Seaways passenger-cargo vessel *Tor Scandinavia* was an imposing sight when viewed from the dockside

On reaching the open deck it was such a relief to breath in fresh air

People were scattered around wrapped in blankets, all wearing bright orange lifejackets — the scene was exactly the same as many a large hotel fire — dark and smoky and the prolonged pungent smell of cables having been burnt through

It was an awesome sight to see the medics being
lowered on to the deck, dangling at the end of a rope

The noise was deafening and the strong down draft
from the blades all but swept the people on deck away

The passenger liner *Prince George* was in dock when smoke was seen. Firefighters eventually stopped pumping water on to the ship and concentrated on saving the dockside. The vessel was allowed to burn itself out

Shipping companies such as Caledonian MacBrayne
(above) who participate in evacuation exercises are to be
congratulated

A new breed of ship — the HSS1500 coming into service in the summer of 1996 will be capable of carrying 1500 passengers and 375 cars. Even bigger vessels are planned

The Scandinavian Seaways passenger-cargo vessel *Tor Scandinavia* was an imposing sight when viewed from the dockside

On reaching the open deck it was such a relief to breath in fresh air

People were scattered around wrapped in blankets, all wearing bright orange lifejackets — the scene was exactly the same as many a large hotel fire — dark and smoky and the prolonged pungent smell of cables having been burnt through

It was an awesome sight to see the medics being lowered on to the deck, dangling at the end of a rope

The noise was deafening and the strong down draft from the blades all but swept the people on deck away

The passenger liner *Prince George* was in dock when smoke was seen. Firefighters eventually stopped pumping water on to the ship and concentrated on saving the dockside. The vessel was allowed to burn itself out

Shipping companies such as Caledonian MacBrayne (above) who participate in evacuation exercises are to be congratulated

A new breed of ship — the HSS1500 coming into service
in the summer of 1996 will be capable of carrying 1500
passengers and 375 cars. Even bigger vessels are
planned

The Scandinavian Seaways passenger-cargo vessel *Tor Scandinavia* was an imposing sight when viewed from the dockside

On reaching the open deck it was such a relief to breath
in fresh air

People were scattered around wrapped in blankets, all wearing bright orange lifejackets — the scene was exactly the same as many a large hotel fire — dark and smoky and the prolonged pungent smell of cables having been burnt through

It was an awesome sight to see the medics being
lowered on to the deck, dangling at the end of a rope

The noise was deafening and the strong down draft
from the blades all but swept the people on deck away

The passenger liner *Prince George* was in dock when smoke was seen. Firefighters eventually stopped pumping water on to the ship and concentrated on saving the dockside. The vessel was allowed to burn itself out

Shipping companies such as Caledonian MacBrayne (above) who participate in evacuation exercises are to be congratulated

A new breed of ship — the HSS1500 coming into service
in the summer of 1996 will be capable of carrying 1500
passengers and 375 cars. Even bigger vessels are
planned

kiosk and fight the fire in the blue hall.

Firemen with breathing apparatus were ordered to enter both corridors to fight the fire. The firemen who went into the starboard corridor were not instructed to check the cabin.

During the evacuation of the passengers, I did not note on a layout plan or list which sections had been evacuated. I relied on my experience. I am completely certain that the evacuation team had reported that the cabins in front of deck 5 in the blue hall had been evacuated. I remember the group gave me the report when I returned to the information hall.

While the evacuation was in progress I did not speak with the bridge or the chief officer about freeing a fire fighting team equipped with breathing apparatus, to assist the catering personnel on deck 5, 6 and 7, even although there was a lot of smoke. This was because I had been informed that all the cabins had been evacuated, except cabins 5001 to 5023, which I informed the bridge about.

The witness concluded his evidence. Then Attorney Arne Engel, appearing on behalf of the ship's owners, proposed that the court hearing be concluded. The maritime court agreed with the proposal and the enquiry closed.

9

COURT FINDINGS

The *Tor Scandinavia* was built in 1976 and it met the requirements applying to passenger ships built at that time. The requirements for ships built at a later date have in many areas been made stricter.

The Danish Maritime Authority found conditions which were open to criticism, also that certain rules in force at the time appeared to be insufficient.

But these conditions were not punishable according to Danish maritime law. And no reason was found to submit to the prosecution service that anyone be charged in connection with the fire.

There were no reasons to disagree with the conclusion of the police investigations which was that the fire had started in a small linen trolley and was most probably started deliberately.

The alarm call to the passengers in the part of the ship which was on fire was considered to be inadequate. This was found to be due to the fire destroying a single loudspeaker unit and putting out of action that entire circuit.

If smoke detectors had been installed in the passenger area, the fire would have been discovered sooner, thus limiting the extent of the fire. Consideration was to be given to install smoke detectors in existing passenger ships, as already applies to new passenger ships.

This fire could only be fought properly using breathing apparatus and although the ship carried the required number of air bottles under current regulation, the supply of air bottles was quickly used up. It was proposed that it should be a requirement that an air compressor, capable of recharging breathing apparatus bottles should be fitted on passenger ships.

As the ship's radio room was put out of action, due to being filled with smoke, it was proposed that the ventilation system of the radio room be separated from the ventilation system of the ship.

The evacuation procedures were inadequate, given the dense smoke.

It was proposed that crew members be required to wear a readily identifiable uniform or some other kind of identification which will clearly mark them as crew members.

This was the substance of the report.

The Marine Accident Investigation Branch in the UK, on reading the report of the enquiry and the findings, noted that a number of points emerged, which were not directly covered or addressed. They were:

1 The general alarm appeared to be operated by push button only, ie, it is not capable of being locked on.
2 The public address and general alarm share the same circuit and when the public address is activated, it cancelled the general alarm.
3 Emergency buttons fitted in passenger cabins appeared to indicate on the fire alarm panel on the bridge, giving rise to confusion.
4 The emergency lights and signs were fitted at deckhead

level, which in the case of dense smoke made them virtually invisible.

5 The evacuation plan seemed to be poorly organised and controlled. To improve the situation, a radical re-appraisal of the plan and practice in its execution was required.

A number of questions were not raised at the Danish maritime court of enquiry. They were:

1 The general alarm to alert passengers of an emergency is by sounding the ship's horn or whistle consisting of seven or more short blasts followed by one long blast. This did not happen.

2 The ship was found to be on fire at 04.55 and the fire was deemed to be completely extinguished at 10.35am. Total time the ship was on fire was five hours and forty minutes. No mention was made of this extraordinarily bad fire.

3 Four hours and five minutes elapsed between the fire being found and a search being made of cabins 5001 to 5023. Two passengers were found to be dead in cabin 5023. No questions were asked about this lengthy delay.

4 It was the duty of a member of the catering personnel to alert and evacuate cabins 5001 to 5023. It was reported to the enquiry that she had 'broken down' and was found sitting on the quarter-deck.

Why were no questions asked about this member of the evacuation team? Was she injured? Or, when she opened the fire door to enter the corridor on deck 5 and seeing the flames and smoke, was she overcome with panic and could not cope with the dangerous situation? It would appear that no one was interested in this person's health and well-being.

Would it have been beneficial to the court if a wider

range of witnesses had been in attendance? We know that the six most senior officers from the ship gave evidence, but what about the 539 passengers, the other 133 members of the crew, a representative from the Danish fire brigade, or a forensic expert?

Very little has been recorded regarding the very important part played by the three German ships during the fatal fire on board the *Tor Scandinavia*. The first ship to arrive at the scene in response to the Mayday was the German vessel *Poseidon*. This ship tied alongside the *Tor Scandinavia* and remained there as an evacuation ship. Had the Abandon Ship command been given, many of the passengers would have been helped to safety by the boarding the *Poseidon*.

The German destroyer *Hamburg* accompanied by the cable ship *Glucksburg* also responded to the Mayday, as did many other vessels. All had altered course to assist the burning ship. In response to an appeal from the captain of the burning ship for firefighters, the captain of *Hamburg* sent a highly skilled team of eleven men. Not only did they extinguish the fire completely, they also recovered the bodies of the two unfortunate Swedish passengers.

After being escorted safely to Esbjerg, the badly damaged *Tor Scandinavia* was repaired in a German shipyard. The total cost was reported in a Swedish newspaper to run to £5million.

10

MORE PASSENGER SHIP FIRES

The *Tor Scandinavia* fire was by no means an isolated incident. Since the beginning of this century, there have been over one thousand fires involving passenger ships worldwide during peacetime.

In 1989, the Marine Accident Investigation Branch (MAIB) was formed to investigate accidents and incidents involving British ships and ships carrying United Kingdom passengers. The MAIB statistics regarding UK passenger ship fires do not make pleasant reading.

Year	Total Number of Fires	Fires on Passenger Ships	% of Passenger Ship Fires
1989	35	3	8.6%
1990	37	5	13.5%
1991	25	7	28%
1992	21	11	52%
1993	12	8	66%
1994	10	6	60%
1995	46	22	48%

These recent figures chart a very disturbing trend. They show that although the number of fires onboard ships was decreasing, the percentage figure for passenger ships has increased at an alarming rate – from 8.6% in 1989, to an astronomical 66% in 1993 and 60% in 1994.

Figures for 1995 show an alarming increase from 10 in 1994 to a frightening 46 last year. The number of passenger ships involved rose from 6 in 1994 to 22 in 1995. Of this total 17 were in fact small fires (eg waste paper bins). But an undetected small fire has the potential of developing quickly into a disaster.

Due to the increase in passenger traffic and many other factors, approximately twenty passenger-carrying ships worldwide will be involved every year in an incident involving fire.

Within seven months of the *Tor Scandinavia* fire, another three passenger ships caught fire within three days of each other. One of these ships was the *Scandinavian Star*. The fire occurred enroute from Oslo to Frederikshaven, Denmark, with 'about 500 passengers' – no one was quite certain of the exact number as no passenger manifest had been left on shore, in contravention of Norwegian laws and the one taken on board had been destroyed by fire.

The ship was completely gutted by fire, with the loss of almost 200 lives. Passengers complained of the following:

February 1991
The huge 74,000 Ton Royal Carribean passenger cruise liner, *Sovereign of the Seas* was docked at San Juan. Puerto Rico, when a fire was discovered in a store on deck five. Over three thousand passengers and crew were evacuated. Fire fighters took over one hour to extinguish the blaze. No injuries were reported. The evacuation was described by local onlookers as alarming.

Confusion reigning amongst the Portuguese and Filipino crew after the fire was discovered.

The same crew were criticized for reverting to their native language in panic and for the lack of help to passengers.

Fire alarm systems in some parts of the ship were not working.

The crew were completely unprepared for the emergency.

Smoke was being distributed throughout the cabins by the air conditioning.

The passengers had to find their own lifejackets.

One of the passengers, Grete Jan Indrehus said, "It was absolute chaos. There was no warning. I was sitting in the top deck saloon when I saw the smoke before any fire alarm sounded. The smoke was coming from the corridors. Anything below deck was a death trap."

Contrary to international laws, some of the lorry drivers were sleeping in the cabins of their vehicles. All were found to be dead.

Mrs Eli Kvale Nielson from Norway said, "I did not hear any alarm. It was terrible. All chaos and no organisation. It was obvious that the crew were not trained for an emergency.

Mr Arvid Rusten, a Norwegian travelling with five children to a table-tennis tournament in Denmark, said, "We saw a lot of smoke and fire. No alarm sounded. The

---

July 1991
The Russian liner *Maxim Gorky* caught fire off the coast of Norway. Seven hundred passengers received the order to abandon ship. Three of the crew lost their lives, one being the ship's hairdresser, a young British girl. Among the passengers were twelve people who had been on board the *Maxim Gorky* when she hit ice three years previously. As a goodwill gesture they had received a reduced fare offer for this cruise.

six of us rushed to the lifeboats and boarded one on the lower deck. After being lowered into the water we were picked up 45 minutes later by a Panamanian ship, given blankets and food, then taken to Sandefjord in Norway."

Police Inspector Johansson said, "There were bodies lying everywhere, many of them children. You can imagine the terrible scenes as they tried to find their way to safety, desperate to find an exit."

The Brittany ferries vessel *Reine Mathilde* was sailing from Caen in France, to Portsmouth, with 600 passengers, 71 crew and 4 service personnel on board. A crewman suffered from smoke inhalation when a fire broke out in the engine room. A 66 year old passenger died after suffering a heart attack, despite the efforts of two doctors to revive him during the blaze.

A Coastguard helicopter was scrambled, to bring one dead and one injured to shore. The tug *Powerful* was diverted to tow the helpless ferry to Portsmouth.

The Italian Costa Company charted the *Fulvia* for cruises to Morroco and the Canary Islands. The ship departed from Genoa on 14th July 1970, carrying 448 passengers and a large crew. At 1.50am a fire was discovered in the engine

---

March 1991

As the cruise liner *Eurosun* sailed to Las Palmas on the Canary Islands, a fire broke out in the early hours of the morning. The weather was settled and the sea was calm as the passengers were alerted to report to their muster station and don life jackets

The captain sent out a Mayday message requesting immediate assistance and ordered the life boats to be swung out in readiness for a mass evacuation of over four hundred passengers

room. The crew were unable to extinguish the fire and a series of small explosions made the situation worse. At 2.35am Commandant Fastings sent out an SOS, calling for immediate assistance.

The passengers, who had been fast asleep, were all huddled on deck, beside the lifeboats, when a massive explosion occurred in the engine room. The captain realised the seriousnes of the situation and gave the order, Abandon Ship. The once happy holidaymakers clambered aboard the lifeboats, which were then lowered into the water where they made their way to the *Anceville*, a ship which had quickly responded to the Mayday message.

Two Spanish tugs attempted to take the now well alight *Fulvia* in tow but after two unsuccessful attempts, the *Fulvia* sank, 35 miles off Tenerife.

The Egyptian ferry *Al-Quurnur-Al-Saudi* was sailing from Jedda in Saudi Arabia, to Safaga in Egypt. The date was May 20, 1994. The ship was carrying 584 passengers. Suddenly a boiler exploded engulfing the ship in flames. In the ensuing panic, hundreds of the frightened passengers jumped overboard.

An American warship picked up survivors from the sea and from an oil rig platform, situated near where the ferry had caught fire. The youngest survivor was a baby

---

and crew. Eighty eight of the passengers were British and a group of them were on a Saga holiday.

Fire fighting teams took one hour to extinguish the fire which had started in the sun lounge. The crew behaved in an orderly and efficient manner, not only in fighting the fire but also in calming the frightened passengers. No injuries were reported. The British Consulate in Las Palmas praised the ship's emergency procedure. Nevertheless, it was a most frightening experience for the passengers and crew.

girl. Her mother, Mrs Safa Youssef had given birth, two hours before the fire had started. Mother and baby reached safety and were treated in hospital. The US navy confirmed that 555 were rescued and 29 had perished.

In the same year, the *Achille Lauro* was sailing off the coast of Somalia, enroute from Genoa to the Sychelles, with over 1000 people on board, when a serious fire broke out. The vast amount of water used in fighting the fire made the ship list dangerously, so dangerously that the Abandon Ship command was given.

Fortunately the weather was fine as the lifeboats were lowered into the water. The rescue operation was controlled by the Rescue Co-ordination Centre at Stavanger, Norway. Three deaths were reported.

The ship blazed away for two days before sinking. This fire put an end to the *Achille Lauro's* chequered career during which she had suffered from three other serious fires in 1965, 1972 and 1981. She had also been involved in a collision in 1975 and had been reached international prominence during a hijack in 1985.

Many of the important factors in averting loss of life were in favour of the *Sally Star*, a Ro-Ro passenger ferry which is registered in the Bahamas. The number of passengers the ship is allowed is 1,754, with a crew of up to 105. The

---

July 1991
The *Starship Majestic* departed from Port Canaveral and was cruising round the Bahamas with eleven hundred passengers. A fire was discovered and the captain issued the order 'Abandon Ship'. Miracuously, no injuries were reported. After the fire was brought under control and extiguished, the vessel was taken in tow and returned to Port Canaveral.

majority of the journeys are with a mix of vehicles and passengers. Other journeys are with commercial vehicles only.

On August 25, 1994 the ship slipped its moorings at the Loon Plage Terminal, clearing Dunkirk Pier head at 2.23am, bound for Ramsgate. The estimated time of the voyage was three hours. All catering and cabin staff were French. The remainder of the crew were British. Two of the commercial vehicles were carrying dangerous goods for which declarations had been submitted. A further 22 freight-carrying vehicles were also on board. Passengers comprised of the 24 vehicle drivers, 4 sub contractors. Total number of non crew was 28, as against the possible 1754 passengers.

Little did they know that two hours later many people would be involved in not only their evacuation but also in fighting a serious fire on board the ship. Among those who became involved that night were HM Coastguard, Dover; off-shore firefighting teams from Kent Fire Brigade; RAF helicopters from Wattisham, Suffolk and from Koksidje, Belgium; a helicopter *India Juliet* from the Solent Coastguard; the RNLI lifeboats at Ramsgate and Margate; as well as tugs and other vessels.

The voyage was uneventful until 4.18am. The second officer was on the bridge when the fire alarm panel indicated a fire in the engine room. The second officer telephoned the fourth engineer, who went to investigate. On opening the forward engine room door, he saw black

February 1992
The French cruise ship *Ocean Pearl* was sailing in the South Pacific when an alarming engine room fire occured. The damage caused put the engine completely out of use. The P&O liner *Sea Princess* responded to the Mayday message, altered course and sailed to the rescue of the three hundred and seventy passengers, thirty seven of whom were British. All were taken to Bali by the *Sea Princess*.

smoke and immediately closed the door.

The deputy master was called to the bridge and permission was given for the main engines to be stopped. The fire alarm panel on the bridge was now indicating fire or smoke on the port side of the main vehicle deck and the engine room. At 4.20am the ship's master was called to the bridge and informed that there was a fire in the engine room.

The general alarm was sounded to alert the passengers and crew. This was followed by an announcement over the public address system. The announcement was short, very short. All that was said was, "Mr Skylight 3 and 4." This in fact was a coded message to the crew. "Mr Skylight" was a message for the fire fighting members of the crew and the numbers 3 and 4 signifies that they were to report to lockers number three and four, where the fire fighting equipment was stored. The fire fighting crew quickly strapped on the breathing apparatus and made their way to the engine room with the fire hose.

On reaching the engine room, they alerted the captain as to the seriousness of the situation. The ship's captain reported to Dover coastguard that his passenger ship had a fire in the engine room and he required immediate assistance from the emergency services. After reporting the ship's position, which was 6.5 miles east of Ramsgate, the captain repeated the Mr Skylight message and sounded the general alarm once more.

Dover Coastguard implemented a well-rehearsed emergency plan which involved three Kent Fire Brigade

---

August 1992

The *Sea Spirit* was cruising off the Norwegian coast when fire broke out in the engine room. The captain decided that the situation was very serious and gave the command Abandon Ship. No injuries were sustained during the evacuation of the one hundred and seventy eight passengers.

appliances being dispatched to Royal Air Force Manston, where the personnel and their equipment would be airlifted by helicopter onto the *Sally Star*. Other appliances were being instructed by Kent Fire Brigade Control, Maidstone, to proceed to Ramsgate where they would be transported by ship.

On board the *Sally Star*, the passengers and non-essential crew were assembled on deck C where they were informed of the fire. The evacuation team were below deck, checking all the cabins. They reported them clear of personnel.

With the main engines stopped, the ship was relying on the two auxiliary generators to supply main electrical power. After they had been running for 22 minutes, both generators stopped. With no power available, the fire pumps also stopped. Just then, the emergency generator started. However two of the fire pumps did not restart. Without all the fire pumps working, the water pressure in the fire hose dropped.

Left with a lack of water to fight the fire, the fire fighting team in the engine room had to make a very hasty exit.

With two of the fire pumps out of action, the firefighters could not control the situation and members of the fire team could not cool down the dangerously hot parts of the ship. The vehicle deck, which is immediately

---

October 1992
The 46,000 ton *Sky Princess* departed from San Francisco with twelve hundred passengers on a cruise to Fort Lauderdale. At 8am, on a position just north of Los Angeles, the passengers were suddenly summoned to their muster stations. They were informed that a fire had been discovered in the ship's cinema. The blaze was contained and no injuries were reported. Less than twenty four hours later, the night manager discovered another fire in the cinema and it was quickly extinguished.

above the engine room, was judged to be overheating. As the situation was now very serious, the captain decided that the passengers and non-essential crew should be transferred to the two RNLI lifeboats which had arrived on the scene.

The evacuation route along which the passengers and non-essential crew were directed meant that they had to pass one of the two vehicles which were carrying dangerous goods. They also had to be led down an open staircase and through dark passageways, guided by the light of torches, held by strategically placed crew members. On reaching G deck, they not only experienced poor visibility but also some smoke from the engine room. They then had to pass through the vehicle deck containing the hazardous chemical cargo, diesel fuel oil and petrol. The engine room fire was immediately below them.

On reaching the pilot door on G deck they were helped aboard the tug *Anglian Riever* which was alongside the *Sally Star* and acting as a platform. From there, they were transferred to the two RNLI lifeboats from Ramsgate and Margate.

The number transported to safety was 102, comprising 85 crew, who were not required for fire fighting and 17 passengers. As they were boarding the two lifeboats, they could see other vessels spraying their fire hoses onto the the outer hull of the *Sally Star* in an attempt to cool it down. They also witnessed the rescue helicopter, R125, arriving

---

August 1993

A massive rescue operation swung into action to save the lives of over five hundred passengers on board the blazing *New Orient Princess*. Three fire fighting ships endeavoured to control the fire, using all their fire hoses to the maximum. Eighteen police launches and a Royal Navy ship came to the rescue of the passengers. Two of the crew were reported injured. The ship had sailed from Hong Kong on an evening gambling cruise.

with the First Strike Fire Team from Kent Fire brigade. By
5.50am all members of the First Strike Fire Team were on
board to assist in the fire fighting. All requests for
additional equipment for this team would be communicated to their own liaison officer who had arrived at Dover
Coastguard.

At 6.18am the rescue helicopter, R 92 arrived on board
with the second team of professional fire fighters and as
they were disembarking from the helicopter, the ship's
captain was requesting Dover Coastguard to monitor his
ship's position in case it drifted into danger.

The 22 Kent fire fighters fought the fire for more than
an hour, until the tug, *Anglian Runner* arrived with a further
8 Kent fire fighters, 3 ambulance staff and additional fire
fighting equipment. With the use of their own portable
fire pumps and with many of the firemen wearing
breathing apparatus, the fire was steadily brought under
control.

At 8.38am, the fire was in fact reported to be under
control and at 11.12am, Dover coastguard received the 'fire
completely out' message.

At the enquiry into this serious sea incident, it
emerged that on departing from Dunkirk, the statutory
safety announcement was given over the public address
system, followed by an example of the warning signal,
which is seven or more short sounds then one long sound.

However the alarm sounded in this emergency bore
no likeness to the warning sounded when the ship was
leaving Dunkirk. It was noted that passengers may have
been tempted to ignore the general alarm sound which in
fact was to warn them that an emergency situation had
occurred. When the muster operation was in progress
difficulties arose, because the crew were not wearing
uniforms or distinctive badges. There was confusion as to
who were crew and who were passengers.

When the emergency lighting was working, many of the bulbs did not light. The general alarm could not be activated continuously without a member of the crew being in attendance. Communication with the firefighters wearing breathing apparatus and control of them required improvement.

These observations were noted and the relevant action was taken by the ship's owners, Sally Line Ltd. This shipping company can be classed as highly responsible, as they are very much involved in joint training between Sally Line staff, HM Coastguard, Kent Fire Brigade, the Royal Air Force and other services.

By coincidence, another ship belonging to the Sally Line had been involved in a joint exercise with all of the above, ten months previously. The exercise had taken place in almost the same location, six and a half miles east of Ramsgate.

Not all incidents of ship fires and how they are responded to are subject to criticism. On Monday April 9, 1990, the passenger ferry *Norrona* was on voyage from Pembroke Dock to Rosslare. Twenty five miles from Pembroke the peace of the bridge was shattered by the strident sound of the fire alarm. The fire panel indicated that the fire was on deck C.

The ship's fire fighting team swung into action and within minutes they had informed the captain of the intensity and enormity of the blaze. Wasting no time, the captain contacted Milford Haven Coastguard, requesting assistance from onshore fire fighters. The coastguard implemented the emergency plan for offshore fire fighting and thereafter controlled the whole operation. Dyfed County Fire Brigade alerted their task force and the first fire fighting team was quickly on their way to assist.

Enroute on the Sea King helicopter R 190, the task force commander was updated by intercom of the ship's present position and the fire situation. Meantime on board the stricken ship, the captain had ordered all 219 passengers to report to their muster stations.

In response to the Mayday, Milford Haven Coastguard had also alerted St David's lifeboat, Fishguard lifeboat, Sea King helicopter 191 from RAF Brawdy and Sea King helicopter 193 from Royal Navy Air Station Culdrose. Sailing to the rescue was the *Bristolian, Arklow Viking, Barmouth* and *Hulda Maersk*.

On board the *Norrona* the ship's firefighting teams were exhausted. They had run out of breathing apparatus bottles and were reduced to covering their faces with wet towels. Their very brave efforts had controlled the fire. They had contained it to an area comprising 32 cabins.

When the Task Force had been lowered onto the ship they were divided into two parties. The first party would strap on their own breathing apparatus and fight the fire. The second party would render much needed first aid to the passengers who were suffering from severe smoke inhalation. A number of the passengers were unconscious and were brought round by the efforts of the Task Force from Dyfed County Fire Brigade.

At this time, a second team comprising six firefighters from Haverfordwest arrived and assisted their colleagues in fire fighting and rendering first aid. A doctor was airlifted onto the ship and after examining the casualties, nine were airlifted to hospital.

When the fire was finally extinguished the final casualty list read, 1 dead, 32 injured. The following was determined: The ship's crew were all well disciplined. The mustering and fire fighting teams were well trained and efficient. Pre-planning for such an incident by all emergency services was well rewarded.

The passenger liner *Prince George* commenced its career cruising the inside passage between Vancouver and Alaska. It then served as a floating hotel in New Westminster, at Expo 86. Three years later, during the infamous Exxon Valdez oil spill, the ship was utilised in Alaska to accommodate the many hundreds involved in the clean-up operation.

In October 1995, the ship was about to commence a new life, as a floating hotel and restaurant, prior to which, it had been hired by a film company who had insured themselves against fire.

On Sunday October 15, 1995, the ship was alongside the dock at Britannia Beach in Canada, when smoke was seen at 3pm. Fire fighters from the towns of Britannia and Squamish were quickly on the scene and were soon pumping water onto the *Prince George*, in an attempt to dowse the fire.

Due to the intensity of the flames and searing heat, no pumps could be activated to pump the water out from the ship and it took a list of eight degrees to starboard. There was a serious danger that the ship would capsize. The fire fighters ceased pumping water onto the ship and concentrated on saving the dockside. The vessel was allowed to burn itself out.

Two weeks later the Canadian Coastguard and the firefighters were still maintaining an around-the-clock vigil at the smouldering remains of what was once a luxury passenger ship. Smoke was still pouring from two of the upper deck vents, preventing fire investigators from boarding the ship. Doug Lucas, the Coastguard Senior Response Officer said, "the *Prince George* is being cremated." The inside of the ship was completely burned out. The exterior was very badly scorched. All the windows were smashed out with the intense heat and the only part of the ship that was unscathed were the lifeboats.

In June 1995, the Eurolink operated ferry *Euromagique* was en route from Sheerness in Kent to the Dutch port of Flushing, when fire broke out in the engine room. The ship was off the Netherlands coast when the incident happened.

Thick black smoke quickly engulfed the vessel. Smoke was even seen pouring out from the vents in the ship's funnel. The top deck was smothered in smoke. Two passing tugs were quickly on the scene and came alongside. A ladder was used to enable the passengers to scramble to safety over the side of the *Euromagique* down onto the open deck of the tugs.

The two tugs and lifeboats rescued the 87 passengers and the 46 crew members. The fire was fought for over an hour before the ship was towed into Flushing, where fire inspectors boarded the damaged vessel to ascertain the cause of the blaze.

In July 1992, the cross channel ferry *Quiberon* was enroute from Plymouth to Roscoff, France. Fifty miles from the French coast, the alarm sounded in the fire panel, indicating a fire in the engine room. The fire fighting team immediately strapped on their breathing apparatus and commenced fighting the blaze.

All passengers were ordered to the main deck to put on their life jackets. A major rescue operation was mounted after a Mayday message for immediate assistance was made by the captain. Eight vessels including HMS *Brecon* altered course to assist the crippled vessel, which was carrying over 1100 passengers, 74 of a crew and 243 cars. Rescue vessels from France also sailed to the assistance.

On shore, an emergency casualty centre with medical staff, social workers and a fleet of ambulances stood by. Meantime, on board the blazing ship, the crew had evacuated all the passengers from the restaurants, cabins, duty free shops and amusement arcades.

Petty Officer Sam Norris was lowered from a helicopter onto the ship to assist in the possible mass evacuation of the passengers.

In the engine room the heat was tremendous and the captain decided to pump monoxide gases onto the fire to completely extinguish the searing flames. The now helpless ship was towed to Roscoff by two French tugs.

During the whole dangerous operation, the crew kept the passengers informed of the on-going situation. Due to the efficient manner in which the crew handled matters, there was no panic, mishaps or injuries among the passsengers, who were praised for remaining calm during their ordeal.

A fire on board a ship is what the crew fear the most. Whether or not there will be casualties is often outwith the control of the crew. But there are many factors over which shipping companies can have control and which will greatly affect the final outcome in the event of fire. Some of these are:

Have some of the crew been involved in firefighting training? When members of the trained crew are on leave, have those replacing them had firefighting training?

Is all the firefighting equipment visually inspected and tested on a regular basis? How many passengers are on board?

What is the position of the ship when the fire is found? For example the *Tor Scandinavia* was a hundred miles from the nearest land. The first rescue vessel took one hour and forty five minutes to reach the burning ship.

11

SMOKERS

140 ferries operate around the UK coast providing almost 90,000 sailings a year. More importantly, they carry 52 million passengers. Where there is a total of 52 million people there are smokers. Where there are smokers, there are careless smokers.

The Marine Safety Agency, an executive agency of the Department of Transport, have found that the most common cause of ship fires is careless smoking. Every year lives are lost and millions of pounds worth of damage is caused because of a single careless act.

Smokers unintentionally cause fires in a number of different ways. For example, when the disco closes at about one o'clock in the morning, a great time has been had by all. The duty free drink has been enjoyed. The cigarette is dangling between fingers; an ash tray is spotted; the cigarette is deposited in the ash tray and:

1 Burns itself out;
2 Slowly burns away until it overbalances and falls onto the carpet;
3 The ash tray is full and the cigarette falls onto the carpet;
4 A passenger bumps against the ash tray and the lit cigarette falls onto the carpet.

In number two, three and four the lit cigarette will smoulder and build up heat. On numerous occasions the cigarette is discarded in a litter bin. The litter bin smoulders for some time before igniting.

In the early hours of the morning the carpet ignites and there is a small fire. All the passengers and most of the crew are asleep. It is between three o-clock and five o-clock in the morning, an ideal time for the fire to spread unchecked. When the fire has built up enough heat and starts to spread, it is then classed as a Good Going Blaze. It is at this point that the heat detector nearest the fire will respond by activating the fire alarm panel in the bridge.

The officer in charge of the ship will then order one of the crew to check the situation and report back, as it could possibly be a false alarm. When the crewman ascertains that there is indeed a fire on board the ship a great deal will now depend on the shipping company and their policy on fire drills and passenger evacuation.

When the Good Going Blaze has been discovered, more problems emerge. If the passenger ship is sailing under a flag of convenience and registered in a country that offers tax incentives, this passenger ship might have a multi-national crew. In the event of an emergency, as stated earlier, people tend to revert to their mother tongue. In this situation total confusion takes over.

NUMAST, the seaman's union, is fighting a constant battle against these lowering of standards in life-saving situations. Serious consideration must be given to the effect that all crew on passenger ships must have a basic knowledge of the English language.

Mr Peter Kerry, Broadstairs, Kent relates,

The ease with which fires start may be illustrated by two occasions during my service, in 1946, on the *Queen Elizabeth*. I was on my way down from the radio room to the tourist dining saloon, walking along one of the long alleyways, when I saw smoke pouring out of a small waste bin. Before I could reach it, a stewardess appeared from out of one of the utility rooms with a jug full of water and extinguished the small fire. The cause was found to be a cigarette. Apparently one of the passengers had used the waste bin as an ash tray.

A few weeks later, a similar small fire occurred again and once more it was put out by a stewardess with a jug of water. According to the stewardess, it was a common occurrence for some passengers to dispose of their cigarettes in this manner. The ship did eventually meet her fate by fire in Hong Kong harbour.

On January 9, 1972 at 10.30am it was reported to the Hong Kong harbour officials that the ship was on fire. The vessel's sophisticated fire precaution system was found to be useless and the fire rapidly spread throughout five of the ship's eleven decks. The fire, now completely out of control, was further assisted when a tank full of diesel oil exploded.

The hundred or so fire fighters from Hong Kong fire brigade were quickly on the scene and they were assisted by the harbour fire boats. Their combined efforts were to no avail as, five hours later, the ship was still burning fiercely. The heat was so intense that the fire fighters had to stop and watch helplessly as the ship took a seventeen degree list. The next day at mid-morning the ship rolled over to starboard and slowly sank.

Mr W Haggarty, a practising solicitor from Ayr, relates,

During November 1990, the Cunard cruise ship *Sagafjord* was sailing from Los Angles to the Panama Canal. The vessel had departed from Puerto Vallanta about 6 o'clock in the evening and was about 25 miles from the Mexican coast.

My wife and I were in bed in our cabin when

we were awakened at 5am by the alarm bells and a succession of blasts on the ship's horn. At first I thought it was a false alarm but on rising and opening the cabin door I could smell smoke. I noticed that the air conditioning was still on in our cabin and as the window onto the promenade deck did not open, I was very conscious of how quickly fire could travel along the alleyway outside our door.

My wife wanted to get dressed before going out but I did not want to take any chance of being trapped in the cabin. I said that we should put on our dressing gowns and get out on deck without any delay. Our boat muster station was right outside our cabin window and we were among the first passengers to arrive at it.

The officer in charge lined the passengers up with the women at the front and the men at the rear. We were then instructed to put on our lifejackets. The ship was still sailing slowly and the sea was calm.

We were informed that there was a fire in C deck, in the crew's quarters. Almost immediately, the lifeboats were lowered down to the promenade deck, ready for evacuation. Most of the passengers were elderly, mainly women. They were obviously nervous but fairly calm outwardly. Having served as a deck officer with the Cunard Group, I suggested to them that as long as the ship was underway, albeit slowly, there would appear to be no immediate likelihood of them having to get into the lifeboats. I explained to them further that because the sea was almost flat calm, they should not find getting into the lifeboats and being lowered, too traumatic.

About this time, a member of the crew was carried out of the door next to us. He was dressed only in shorts and his body was completely black with smoke.

From time to time, the captain broadcast a report on how the fire fighting was progressing and about 7am, he announced that the fire was now under control. The catering staff, who were mixed European, served us with fruit juices and croissants at our boat muster station. One hour later it was announced that the fire was out and that we could now stand down.

Throughout the time everyone that I could see was taking everything very calmly. I understand that this was the general attitude of the passengers throughout the emergency. We left our muster station and were informed that coffee, rolls and croissants would be made available in the lido deck. We all went along there still wearing our lifejackets, pyjamas, dressing gowns and various other modes of attire. In no time, there was quite a party atmosphere. As we discussed the emergency and enjoyed our breakfast, the sun came up.

That evening in the dining room, when the captain came to his table he received a standing ovation from the passengers. He in turn expressed his greatest admiration for the manner in which the passengers had conducted themselves throughout.

The gymnasium and the spa on deck C were destroyed and many cabins on B deck were for some days, out of use. The cause of the fire was apparently a member of the crew falling asleep with a cigarette still lit.

On Monday 26 February 1996, the Cunard owned *Sagefjord* once more experienced a fire. The ship had departed from Fort Lauderdale, Florida in early January on a 90-day world cruise. The 476 passengers including 62 Britons had paid an average of £16,000 for the once-in-a-lifetime voyage.

Fifty three days into the cruise, the Nassau registered ship was en route from Hong Kong to Kota Kinabalo in Malaysia. At 2am a fire broke out in the engine room. The fire was so severe it left the luxury liner drifting helplessly in the South China Sea. A Mayday message was giving the ship's position 200 miles off the Phillipines coast. The captain requested the assistance of tugs to tow the ship to Subic Bay, a former US naval base, sixty miles from Manila. None of the passengers or any of the 300 crew were injured and all remained on board while the liner was under tow, even though the engine and main generators were out of action.

Cunard offered to fly their passengers home. Those who wished to continue their cruise holiday were offered a choice of a berth on the *QE2* or the *Royal Viking Sun*. A Cunard spokesperson said, "Passenger comfort and safety is our prime concern and we are doing everything we can to ensure our passengers are looked after in the way they would expect."

What happened to the passengers who decided to continue their cruise on the *Royal Viking Sun* has to be a unique experience in bad luck. They were completely unaware that they were sailing into trouble yet again. On Sunday 5 April the luxury liner was sailing in the Red Sea and, as widely reported in the press, ran aground on a coral reef and was holed below the water line.

13

EVACUATION

A report in July 1995 from the all-party Commons Select Committee on Transport found that 70% of passenger ferries using UK ports failed to meet current international safety standards. The MPs are critical of evacuation procedures and the lack of buoyancy aids on ships to keep them afloat in the event of an accident. They are also worried about difficulties involved in the lowering of lifeboats once ships list further than 15 degrees.

Passenger ships are increasing in size. P&O Princess Cruises took delivery in December 1995 of the 76,500 gross tonne *Sun Princess*. This is the largest passenger ship in the world. A sister ship, *Dawn Princess* will follow in 1997. The maximum capacity for these ships will be 2,400 with a crew of 900. In 1998, P&O will take delivery of the *Grand Princess*. This 100,000 gross tonne passenger ship will carry a total of more than 3,700 passengers and crew. The passenger ship industry envisage even larger ships of 160,000 gross tonnes which will carry over 4,000 passengers and crew.

These immense passenger ships with long continuous multi-deck arrangements, large halls and spacious shopping malls could pose major fire and escape problems. Evacuation of such vessels may be likened to the evacuation of a small town having restricted means of escape which must be completed within 30 minutes.

Should fire break out, a rapid response to contain and extinguish the fire and to prevent the passage of smoke through the vessel is crucial. Smoke logged escape routes and muster stations could be a serious hazard to safe evacuation. Careful assessment of these risks must be undertaken at the design stage so that appropriate measures are taken to reduce them.

For example, fire and smoke surveillance and control systems monitored and operated from a safety control centre should ensure early detection of the fire and its isolation. Simplified ventilator damper arrangements and computer aided control of ventilation systems will assist in preventing the spread of smoke to other spaces.

However, well trained officers and crew as well as hi-tech design solutions are required if the risk of fire and smoke are to be reduced to an acceptable level.

A heavy burden is therefore placed on the officers and crews to maintain a highly disciplined safety organisation. A Safety Officer heading a team responsible for the maintainance of all safety equipment and the training of all personnel in fire fighting and evacuation procedures is considered essential. Continuous training and development of crew, some of whom are multi-lingual and not necessarily professional seamen, is critical in ensuring success of the safety system on board all passenger ships.

Compared to the 15,000 tonne *Tor Scandinavia* the new breed of passenger ships can only be described as massive and could be likened to a Butlins holiday camp afloat. In the event of a fire, the evacuation of over 4,000 passengers and crew does not bear thinking about. A repeat of the terrible tragedy in December 1987, when the Philippine ferry *Dona Paz* caught fire and an estimated 2,000 perished,

110

must not be allowed to happen.

Many passenger ferry companies do not become involved with evacuation training with passengers, unlike the cruise ships which always involve passengers. Two regular passengers on the *QE2* were of the opinion that the fire drills were in need of improvement as the passengers became anxious making their way to their allocated lifeboat station. This was because they were at one end of the ship and their lifeboat station was at the other end. This led to a situation where passengers were passing many lifeboat stations to reach their allocated one, with those at the bow of the ship making their way to the stern and those at the stern making their way to the bow.

Evacuation training is very important and should involve passengers. Shipping companies who are apprehensive about involving passengers could involve 'volunteers' as did the Stena Line on their ship evacuation exercise referred to in an earlier chapter.

When the Abandon Ship order is given, the captain has decided that the passengers will be safer evacuating the ship rather than remaining on board. In 1983 the International Maritime Organisation completely rewrote chapter three of their Safety of Life at Sea (SOLAS) book to ensure that everyone on board a ship involved in an accident can be evacuated within 30 minutes.

How was this time limit of 30 minutes arrived at? The thinking behind it is based on the assumption that a ship carrying say, 1800 passengers/crew would have six muster areas. That would mean that at each muster area there should be 300 people. 300 volunteers are invited onboard and they are evacuated from one muster station on the ship in 30 minutes. In theory this means that 6 times 300 can be evacuated safely in the same time.

The strange thing is that this 30 minute 'safe time limit' had never been tested for 1800 people, far less for

4000 passengers and crew. That is until the House of Commons Transport Select Committee called for an evacuation exercise to take place. The committee requested that the evacuation was to be as realistic as possible.

Captain N R Pryke, Head of Safety on the Stena Line offered to make a ship available to the UK Marine Safety Agency for the exercise and had no hesitation in agreeing to the use of the *Stena Invicta*. Captain Cory, Captain Weston and the entire crew were involved.

On 13 January 1996 the evacuation exercise took place, not in the high seas or mid-way in the North Sea, but in the sheltered Western Dock of Dover Harbour. The Full Alert simulation was watched by press and national safety observers. The cross channel passenger ship *Invicta* was berthed when the exercise took place and 800 volunteer passengers were evacuated from the 19,763 tonne Stena Line ferry.

The requested 'realistic as possible' evacuation commenced when it was announced to the passengers that there was a serious fire on board and the Abandon Ship order was given. The 40 feet special escape chutes were secured to the ship and lowered into life rafts. Two of the life rafts failed to inflate properly.

At the 30 minute point when evacuation should have been complete, only an estimated 315 were clear of the ship. The exercise, even although carried out in a calm harbour, took more than double the stipulated time to complete. The slow evacuation was blamed on the caution of the volunteers.

The £70,000 exercise held in the haven of Dover harbour had many advantages to the passenger ships which can encounter really rough weather and stormy seas. As for the 800 volunteers, how can 800 be compared to the 2000 passengers and 900 crew carried at present? What about the year 1998 when between 4,000 and 5000 passengers and crew are aboard?

The 30 minute time limit for the complete evacuation of a passenger ship may have been acceptable when ships were capable of carrying far fewer passengers. It is now long overdue to assess the acceptable time for the complete evacuation of ships. A realistic time limit will act as a brake on the ever larger size of passenger ships – scale must surely be about cost-effectiveness taking priority over all other considerations including safety.

Future safety requirements dictate that evacuation exercises should be held on a very regular basis. Shipping companies Stena Line, Caledonian MacBrayne and all those who participate in exercises with the use of their ships are to be congratulated.

Passengers should also be forewarned on when and how to abandon ship, entering the water and what to do when in the water.

Preparing to Abandon Ship

On hearing the sounding of the alarm and seven or more short blasts followed by one long blast on the ship's whistle, do not panic. Put on plenty of warm clothing. Woolly clothing is best and as many layers as possible. Put on your life jacket and proceed to your muster station. Do not waste time – final adjustments to clothing and to your life jacket may be made on the way to the muster station or after arrival there.

Abandon Ship

Abandon ship only when told to do so. When the order is given, enter the lifeboats or liferafts at the embarkation deck. This will keep you dry.

Entering the water

If it is necessary to enter the water, choose a suitable place from which to leave the ship. Beware of the drift of the ship, the position of survival craft in the water and other hazards such as burning oil. Do not jump into the water unless it is essential. However if you have to, cross you arms in front of you and block your nose and mouth with one hand. Keep your feet together, look straight ahead (do not look down) and jump feet first.

When in the water

Avoid remaining in the water for one second longer than is necessary. Get into a survival craft as soon as possible, otherwise get clear of the ship. Do not swim aimlessly as this increases body heat loss. Float as still as possible in your life jacket as swimming increases heat loss. Activate the life jacket light (yes, it has one) and blow the whistle attached to your life jacket to attract attention. If possible form a group with other survivors in the water. Keep you knees up to your chest to lessen body heat loss.

14

THE MARINE SAFETY AGENCIES

Four large passenger ships involved in fires within a seven month period in 1989/90 required serious consideration to existing safety rules and on 15 June 1990, the International Maritime Organisation Sub-Committee on Fire Protection held a meeting to discuss Fire Protection Systems for Passenger Ship Safety.

The safety representatives from Denmark submitted the view:

> Recent fire casualties in passenger ships has in a tragic way demonstrated that the regulations for the protection against fire and the operational fire fighting readiness do not provide a satisfactory level of safety.

There was a recognition from other countries that regulations were inadequate and were not properly applied. Other items on the agenda included discussion of a number of recent passenger ship fires where the crews' performance during fire emergencies had been inadequate.

There was a general recognition that on board personnel should receive training and drills to become well versed in firefighting and fire safety measures. The common practice of transferring crew members from one ship to another at frequent intervals meant that without onboard training and drills, they may not become sufficiently familiar with the fire safety features on the ship which they are serving.

But who are the agencies in Britain who have a responsibility to look after passenger safety?

Marine Accident Investigation Branch (MAIB)

The Marine Accident Investigation Branch was established in 1989 and like the Coastguard, is highly regarded in the shipping industry. It is a separate branch within the Department of Transport. All inspectors are qualified in one of the three marine disciplines – nautical, engineering and naval architecture. They lecture on accident investigation to a number of marine interest organisations and at training courses sponsored by the International Maritime Organisation.

The primary function of the inspectors is to invest-igate accidents and incidents involving UK registered vessels worldwide, or involving any ship in UK waters. An accident involves loss of life, serious injury or when a person is lost overboard. It also covers damage to a ship, stranding, collision and abandonment.

An incident is classed as a near-miss, in other words, when an accident almost happened. There are three levels of investigation, depending on how serious the accident or incident.

An administrative inquiry involves less serious cases. Enquiries are made by letter or telephone without the need for a visit. An inspector's investigation is for more serious cases. When feasible, the ship is visited and witnesses interviewed. For major incidents a comprehensive inspector's enquiry is held, usually involving a team of inspectors. In all cases, the inspectors have the authority to consider evidence from as many sources as possible. When necessary, technical advice will be sought from outside the branch. An objective report is then produced and will be released when there are important lessons to be learned. The findings into the cause of accidents often lead to recommendations to prevent similar accidents in the future.

Some 2,000 accidents/incidents are reported each year. Almost 600 require investigation by the MAIB and of these some 100 are deemed serious enough for an inspector's investigation. When foreign ships carrying British passengers are involved in incidents, including fires, the MAIB requests copies of the findings. After the findings are studied, the MAIB add their own observations and comments.

International Maritime Organisation (IMO)

It has long been recognised that action to improve safety at sea would be more effective if carried out at an international level rather than individual countries implementing safety rules without the cooperation of others. A conference held in 1948 by the United Nations established the inter-governmental Maritime Consultative Organisation. In 1982 the name was changed to the International Maritime Organisation. One of the sub-committees of this body was formed to specialise in fire protection. The first international maritime safety conference organised was in 1960 and regulations covering all aspects of shipping safety were adopted and named Safety of Life at Sea (SOLAS) and a book of that name covering all regulations was issued. These regulations came into force in 1965.

Over the years many of the regulations were amended in response to new developments but as with much international legislation there are difficulties in making rules binding. The current membership comprises around 145 contracting states.

Royal National Lifeboat Institution (RNLI)

The RNLI is a registered charity which exists to save life at sea. It is the world's oldest lifeboat service and since its foundation in 1824, more than 127,000 people have been saved. Today, as one of the UK's and the Republic of Ireland's essential services, it provides lifeboat cover up to 50 miles off the coast.

Lifeboat men and women are volunteers, based at over 200 stations round the British and Irish coast. The RNLI is a charity which depends entirely on contributions from the public to meet its £60million annual running costs.

Marine Safety Agency (MSA)

The Marine Safety Agency, formerly the Surveyor General's Organisation, was established as an executive agency within the Department of Transport in April 1994. The MSA is responsible for implementing the Government's strategy for marine safety and prevention of pollution from ships. The overall aim is to develop, promote and enforce the highest standards of marine safety and to minimise the risk of pollution from ships.

Among their very many other duties, the MSA carry out inspections on British and foreign registered ships using British ports. These inspections include the firefighting and fire prevention equipment to ensure they meet the statutory requirements and that they are in good working order.

International Chamber of Shipping

The International Chamber of Shipping, founded in 1921, is the worldwide organisation of ship owners and ship managers.

British Chamber of Shipping

Founded in 1878, the British Chamber of Shipping is the organisation of British ship owners and managers.

The Coastguard

The Coastguard Agency, often referred to as the Coastguard or HM Coastguard, is Britain's maritime emergency response organisation. It exists to minimise loss of life at sea and on the coasts of the UK. The Coastguard's use of sophisticated technology is matched by the professional expertise and local knowledge of its officers, all of whom have had maritime experience.

In a maritime emergency the Coastguard calls on and co-ordinates all available facilities including the Royal National Lifeboat Institution (RNLI), Royal Air force, Royal Navy, the Ministry of Defence, other aircraft and ships. The Coastguard would also involve their own helicopters, general purpose boats and cliff rescue teams. In the event of the emergency being a ship on fire, the Fire Brigade would be called to render assistance.

On shore, the injured, dead, bereaved and bewildered have to be tended to. First aid, food, accommodation, information to relatives and much more all have to be organised. To assist, local authority emergency planning, social work department, Fire Brigade, Police, Port Authority, hospitals and the Ambulance service would all have to be co-ordinated by the Coastguard. The area they cover is around the 10,500 mile coast line of Britain and

1000 miles into the North Atlantic.

One of the biggest concerns must be the distinct possibility of a serious fire involving a ship with 2,000 or more passengers. Include the risk factor of serious injuries, night time, choking fumes, severe weather conditions and the trauma of evacuation. This combination of circumstances has happened many times in the past and is waiting to happen again. HM Coastguard takes the possibility of another passenger ship disaster very seriously.

If and when this disaster does occur, the Coastguard will be in a position to maintain their well earned reputation of being not only the most modern maritime service in Europe but also one of the most efficient. Continual training and the appointment of a Ferry and Merchant Shipping Liaison Officer, in 1992, is the way the Coastguard have prepared themselves for almost any maritime emergency.

Passenger ferry search-and-rescue seminars are held on a regular basis. Participating are all those already mentioned plus shipping companies.

Three such exercises were held in the West of Scotland, where more than eight million passengers travel to and fro annually. The first was Operation Clansman. The passenger ship involved was from the Caledonian MacBrayne fleet. All services were involved in evacuating passengers by means of helicopter and lifeboats.

The second was Exercise Beauforts Dyke where HM Coastguard Clyde, HM Coastguard Belfast, the RNLI, 819 Naval Air Squadron, 72 Squadron RAF, Emergency Planning from Belfast, Strathclyde Police, Fire Brigade and many more were all involved. These type of exercises are extremely expensive but very essential.

The third such exercise in the West of Scotland was Operation Neptune, a very important paperwork exercise with emergency personnel and Strathclyde Fire Brigade in attendance. It was designed to study the combined response to a ferry accident. All of these exercises are invaluable to all those involved in maritime rescue operations, including ship owners.

All major exercises involve realistic scenarios, some including ferry fires. The Coastguard has a commitment to hold six major live exercises a year to test contingency plans for search and rescue incidents, particularly those involving ferry fires. Each district has the authority to hold smaller exercises, some of which would be realistic and some on paper.

The realistic ones would include the use of a ship from one of the ferry owners. It would involve all emergency services and the whole operation would be completely co-ordinated by the Coastguard. The paper exercises involve representation from all emergency services being brought together and confronted with a maritime emergency. An in-depth discussion would follow as to the action each service would take. At the close of the meeting a date will be arranged for a follow up meeting where all the representatives put forward any additional ideas on action which should or should not be taken.

So, in summary, the Marine Accident Investigation Branch investigate ship fires and the International Maritime Organisation oversee safety regulations across the world. The Marine Safety Agency keep a watching brief on firefighting procedures and the RNLI and the Coastguard respond to the emergencies as they arise. There is a feeling however that there is far too much involvement from shipping owners in safety regulations made by the IMO.

This feeling is strengthened by the fact that ship owner organisations like the British Chamber of Shipping sit in on safety conferences and are allowed to give an input on fire safety policy. The question arises, should shipping owners be allowed such a role in making the regulations for passenger safety?

If a new hotel is in the process of being designed and built, who do we put in charge to ensure maximum fire safety for the public? The professional fire brigade, of course, who have all the expertise. They also have a fire prevention department.

What could be more sensible than to have the fire brigade in charge of fire prevention and fire fighting equipment on board passenger vessels?

The fire brigade have the legal authority to visit annually, guest houses and hotels, to inspect the fire fighting equipment smoke detectors and emergency lighting systems. When new regulations are implemented, the hotel and guest houses have to update their equipment.

The anomalies surrounding fire safety regulations on land and at sea are brought into sharp focus by the case of *Arctic Penguin*, one of the world's last existing iron sailing ships. The vessel has been fully restored and operates as a visitor attraction and museum and is permanently moored in the harbour of the busy little Argyllshire village of Inveraray on Loch Fyne. As a static museum within the area of their jurisdiction, the local fire brigade of course carry out an annual inspection of the firefighting equipment and the ship complies with all regulations. The staff are acquainted with evacuation rules and procedures. Should they be required, the fire brigade would be on board within minutes, due to the close proximity of the local fire station.

If however *Arctic Penguin* were to leave the safety of the harbour, the situation would drastically change as the fire brigade would no longer have jurisdiction over fire safety on a moving ship. Professional firefighters would no longer be allowed to carry out their annual inspection and the ship would be covered by the Safety of Life at Sea (SOLAS) regulations.

The Marine Safety Agency have the responsibility of ensuring that fire fighting equipment on board passenger ships is in good working order. Yet because their primary area of expertise is not in professional firefighting, their judgment on fire safety matters must surely be open to question.

One of the most out of date rules, for example, is the Merchant Shipping (Fire Protection) Regulation 1984 which stipulates that,

> Passenger ships should have four breathing apparatus sets. These can be either four self-contained breathing apparatus (similar to sub-aqua divers') or two self contained and two smoke hoods.

The smoke hood is exactly what the name implies. It is a hood with a visor, a set of bellows and thirty six metres of hose. The hose connects the hood to the bellows. The idea is for the wearer to put on the hood to enable him safely to enter the smoke-filled area, while someone in the smoke free area pushes the bellows to provide the fresh air supply.

There are many safety reasons why fire brigades replaced the smoke hood forty years ago. One is that the wearer can only walk the length of the hose. Should there be someone in difficulty two metres further away, then they could not be reached. Also, should the person pumping the bellows be engulfed in smoke then pumping would have to cease, thus endangering the life of the wearer of the hood. With self-contained breathing apparatus, the wearers will always work in pairs.

A professional firefighter input into fire safety matters

at sea would mean that this particular Shipping Regulation would be changed immediately and the smoke hoods would be housed in maritime museums.

So the question is a very live one – should the Marine Safety Agency be implementing regulations for our safety or would it not be much more sensible to allocate the task to professional fire brigades?

15

WHAT NEEDS TO BE DONE

A New Breed of Ship

The summer of 1996 will see in an entirely new passenger ship. The HSS 1500 will be capable of carrying 1,500 passengers and 375 cars or 100 cars and 50 commercial vehicles. The length of the ship is 120 metres and the width is 40 metres, the same size as a football pitch. The speed it is capable of is an astounding 40 knots, double the speed of the conventional ferry.

Passenger facilities are almost unique. There are spacious air conditioned lounges, restaurants, bars, duty free and tax free shops, video lounges with the latest interactive computer games. There will be play rooms for children and during summer months there will be live entertainment.

The ship's appearance is completely different from conventional ferries – it could be described as a huge catamaran. The method of propulsion and manoeuvring is also different – instead of propellers four massive water jets power the ship .

Stena Line have installed in the HSS, 250 smoke detectors. Should one or more be activated a 'High Fog System' would become operational. This is a high pressure spray of water which would extinguish the fire before it goes out of control – in other words, a very sophisticated sprinkler system. The evacuation procedure of the HSS is similar to an aircraft evacuation. When the aircraft has landed and the passengers have to be evacuated, it is by means of a chute. With the HSS, the chute would lead into one of the lifeboats.

Safety Training

At present, there is no hard and fast rule laid down by the shipping owners as to what percentage of the crew must attend fire fighting courses.

On the *Tor Scandinavia*, only five of the crew were in attendance at the fire muster station. Five, out of a crew of 135. The ship was in the middle of the North Sea, a hundred miles from the nearest land

By contrast Western Ferries, operating in the West of Scotland, have always been conscious that one of the greatest hazards of the sea is fire aboard a ship. As a result, all their staff have attended special courses designed by the fire brigade. Half of the seafaring staff attended an intensive four day course on fire fighting and damage control. The other half of the seafaring staff attended a comprehensive two day course on fire fighting. There is no legal obligation to do this but the company arranged the courses for the benefit of their passengers and the safety of their ships and crew.

There are an adequate number of fire fighting training establishments strategically placed throughout the UK. All passenger ship key personnel and a percentage of the crew should attend these courses and attend refresher courses every three years.

Ship owners freely admit that they move personnel from ship to ship as demands dictate. This could lead to a situation where only a small number of a ship's crew have attended a fire fighting training course. Most key personnel do attend courses but when do they attend refresher courses? One senior officer admitted that he did attend a course but it was eighteen years ago.

All NUMAST members, while training for their certificates of competency, receive specialist fire fighting training from professional fire fighters. The International Maritime Organisation should stipulate that no less than 25% of a ship's crew should be in possession of a valid certificate from an approved firefighting training course. Those holding a certificate should be under obligation to attend a refresher course every five years.

Safety Policy

Caledonian MacBrayne sail to twenty three Scottish Islands. In the summer months they sail from Ardrossan to the Isle of Man. In 1994 they carried 6.2 million passengers and 1.5 million vehicles. The company has an excellent relationship with the Coastguard Agency.

The Marine Superintendent of this shipping company is the safety adviser who develops and revises, where necessary, the organisation and arrangements for implementing safety policy. He carries out regular and random checks. He also reports at least once a year to the board on the operational safety policy. The board review and as necessary revise the policy in the light of the report.

Caledonian McBrayne's safety policy of appointing a designated Marine Superintendent with responsibility for all aspects of safety should be adopted by all members of the International Maritime Organisation.

Fire Hose

The International Maritime Organisation rules do not specify the length of fire hose. A number of shipping companies carry fire hose which are ridiculously short. During the *Tor Scandinavia* emergency a member of the crew had to double backwards and forwards, to fetch two additional lengths of hose from another part of the ship to enable the fire fighters to reach the fire. Valuable time was lost in a very serious situation, when every minute counts. The standard length of fire hose should be twenty metres.

The fire brigade dispensed with canvas firefighting hose twenty years ago, replacing it with rubber lined hose. The reason was that the canvas hose must be dried out completely every time it is used, otherwise it will perish. When next used the weakened canvas hose is liable to burst, rendering it virtually useless. Valuable time is then spent not only closing down the firefighting water supply but also replacing the burst hose.

Shipping companies should follow the example of the fire brigade and replace all canvas hose with the rubber lined type. Particular attention should be paid to the maintenance of hose couplings. Without proper maintentance couplings will not operate, thereby rendering the fire hose useless.

Lifejackets

Having travelled on numerous passenger-carrying ships over a period of thirty years we have never been shown how to put on a lifejacket and we have never been informed as to where they are stored.

In contrast, every time we travel by plane, a demonstration is given on how to don a lifejacket, how to tie it firmly, how to inflate it, how to top it up with air if required, how and when to use the whistle which is attached and we are advised where the lifejackets are kept.

The safety demonstration which is given on every aircraft should also be given on passenger-carrying ships.

The timetable issued by Western Ferries contains safety instructions. This is an excellent idea which should be implemented by all shipping companies. The instructions pertaining to lifejackets reads,

> Lifejackets are carried for all those on board,
> including small lifejackets for children.
> Please read the instructions on how to fit them
> on and note the clearly marked stowage
> positions.
> The early issue of lifejackets is a prudent safety
> precaution and does not necessary mean that
> you will have to abandon ship.

These few simple words printed on the back of a ferry timetable tell us a great deal.

1 They inform us that there are two sizes of lifejackets. Had we not been made aware of this, then in an emergency, we very well might have strapped an adult lifejacket onto a child. In the event of the child entering the water, the adult lifejacket might prove to be utterly useless.

2 They advise the passengers to read the instructions on how to put on a lifejacket.

3 The passengers are also advised to note where the lifejackets are stored.

4 The message allays fears "that should the order be given, it is a precautionary measure and does not necessary mean that the passenger has to abandon ship."

5 The passenger is made aware that lifejackets are carried for everyone.

This last point is very interesting as it assures the

passengers that there are lifejackets for all. The maritime safety authority in America implemented a law in 1995 that states, "All vessels must carry a lifejacket for each person on board." This law should be implemented in Great Britain and should include not only British registered ships but all ships sailing to or from the United Kingdom.

Sprinkler Systems

It should be noted that in the event of a sprinkler system being activated due to a build-up of heat, it is only at one outlet in the whole system that the water comes from. If that one outlet fails to contain the fire then another outlet is activated and so on.

On the *Queen Elizabeth* we know that the catering lady extinguished a fire by pouring a jug of water on it. This is exactly the same as a sprinkler system. Another example is the smoker falling asleep in his or her cabin. Should the cigarette start a small fire then the sprinkler outlet in that cabin is activated. If the fire spreads out of control into the corridor, then the nearest outlet in the corridor is activated. In other words, every outlet on the ship is not activated drenching every one because of a small fire.

It is a legal requirement of all UK hotels that a sprinkler system is fitted and maintained in good working order. The new high speed ships from the Stena Line are fitted with sprinkler systems. It is now time for all passenger ships to have sprinkler systems fitted.

Passenger Ship Fire Safety Panel

A panel of experts should be in charge of implementing regulations regarding fire safety on passenger ships in this country. The panel should comprise:

        three members of HM Coastguard including their

WHAT NEEDS TO BE DONE

Ferry and Merchant Shipping Liaison Officer;
the Safety Officer from the National Union of
Marine, Aviation and Shipping Transport
Officers (NUMAST);
four representatives from the fire brigade;
two representatives from the Marine Accident
Investigation Branch (MAIB);
three members of the Marine Safety Agency (MSA);
and three members of the International Maritime
Organisation.

Without doubt, the above could not be classed as
anything other than experts on fire safety on passenger
ships. The above committee should have overall responsibility to stipulate the fire prevention and fire fighting
equipment ships must carry. This committee should meet
no less than four times per year.

The fire brigade should have the authority to board
ships and inspect fire prevention and fire fighting
equipment.

The following should no longer have any jurisdiction
regarding regulations pertaining to fire safety and
evacuation other than ensuring that the regulations are
strictly adhered to:
The International Chamber of Shipping;
The British Chamber of Shipping;
Ship Owners and Ship Managers.

British Fire Brigades
At present a number of fire brigades are very much
involved with the Coastguard and a few ship owners
regarding the training of fire brigade personnel to ensure
that they are conversant with maritime fire fighting,
including:
On board-ship-fire fighting exercises;

131

Helicopter exercises including being lowered onto ships;

What fire fighting equipment would be required.

Now is the time for legislation to be passed that all fire brigades covering coastal areas should be trained in maritime fire fighting.

16

STATEMENTS

Very many people have contributed their time and expertise in the preparation of this book. There is a common thread amongst mariners of concern for safety at sea. Some of the arguments made in the preceding pages have been informed and shaped by some of those quoted below. It's as well to allow those who made these statements to speak for themselves.

Fire at sea – the Ship Captain's Nightmare
Captain Ted Fields
Captain Fields is a freelance nautical consultant. He served at sea from 1946 and in later years has acted as a marine advisor.

> Fire at sea is frightening. On a Class I liner there is a risk of passenger casualties. There is however an even more significant risk for passengers on ferries.
>
> The Merchant Shipping Acts catergorise passenger ferries on short international voyages and some coastal routes as Class II vessels. This group includes the Ro-Ro ferries, which in addition to their high fire risk have the added disadvantage

of quick capsize if water gets onto the car deck.

Class I passenger vessels, the usually large ocean going liners and cruise ships, have a much better safety record than the ferries in the context of fire.

The 1894 Merchant Shipping Act introduced measures to improve safety of life at sea. This was a significant step forward. Subsequently further improvements were introduced as experience highlighted deficiencies. The introduction of lifeboat capacity for all on board following the loss of the *Titanic* in 1912 was a striking example. Regrettably this innovation was not extended to Class II ships.

As we come to the end of the millennium there appears to be a different outlook on safety of life at sea. Since the 1970s when the government department responsible for marine safety became technically rather than professionally orientated, economy has superseded safety as the norm.

The reluctance of the International Maritime Organisation and our own Marine Safety Agency to deal expeditiously with the ever increasing number of ferry casualties bodes ill for the next century.

Fire drill, usually in conjunction with boat and other emergency drills, are by law required to be practised weekly on passenger vessels. On Class II ships the normal procedure is to carry out the drills when there are no passengers on board. Class I ships on the other hand carry out the drills with passengers on board – indeed the passengers are involved in the drills.

Class I ships are also required by law to hold a drill for passengers within 24 hours of embarkation. Class II ships are only required to make a safety announcement on sailing. Ferry passengers are usually too busy trying to get a seat or looking for the cafeteria or duty free shop to listen to the safety announcement. Because they are on board longer the Class I ship passengers become familiar with the layout on board and know where to go and what to do in an emergency. They also have the added advantage of knowing where their lifejacket is and how to put it on.

Undoubtedly an important factor from the point of view of safety of life in the event of a fire on board is the ratio of crew to passengers. The QE2 for example carries 1750 passengers and has 1025 crew. On the other hand there are cross channel ferries carrying 2200 passengers with crews of about 100.

In the event of a fire at least 20 of the crew will form fire-fighting parties. In the Class II ship this will leave about 80 personnel to look after the passengers. Some of the crew members will be detailed to attend passengers in wheelchairs. It is totally impractical to expect the remainder of the crew to equip some 2000 people with lifejackets, man the lifeboats and liferaft equipment and indeed evacuate the ship in thirty minutes required by law.

There is an above average incidence of fire on Class II ships. Cutting crew numbers to a minimum is a major factor. Most of the fires start in machinery spaces and the lack of cleanliness is significant. Tight schedules mean the machinery is in use almost 24 hours a day with little time to do even minor maintainance. There is still a dependance on water as a firefighting medium on Ro-Ro ferries. A small amount of that water coming on to the car deck would quickly introduce negative stability and capsize.

The International Maritime Organisation introduces a large number of regulations. However in countries such as India, Pakistan and the Phillipines these regulations are administered by local officials. They should be regulated by the IMO to ensure that they are strictly adhered to. The IMO should comprise more safety professionals and less representation from shipping companies.

The Marine Safety Agency is responsible for

135

issuing passenger certificates to Class I and II ships. Unfortunately that agency has a preponderance of people in the field with little or no sea-going experience. The Agency is issuing passenger certificates to ships which do not meet the standards required by the Merchant Shipping Acts. The disclosure in November 1994 that many of our Class II ferries had leaking bow doors and later that year the *QE2* fiasco must not go unchallenged. As a maritime nation we deserve better.

Dave Jardine-Smith, HM Coastguard Ferry and Merchant Shipping Liaison Officer

At present local authority Fire Brigades are not obliged to become involved in maritime fire fighting and rescue operations. The ideal situation would be if we could rely on 100% support from all UK Fire Brigades as not only do they have the professional expertise, they also have the special-ised cutting equipment which can be utilised on board ships when required.

Liverpool Labour Euro MP Mr Ken Stewart, a former seaman

It is just beyond words, there seems to have been a bad lack of security. We in the European Market have been seeking action ever since the *Herald of Free Enterprise* disaster, but nothing seems to have happened. International regulations are nowhere near as tough as they should be and I would like to see increased EC powers.

1995 House of Commons Transport Select committee stated,
> Safety measures on ferries are inadequate and most passengers could not be evacuated safely.

International Maritime Organisation
> Loss of life at sea has become unacceptable, International safety rules are under constant threat from the action of some states.   (1992)

National Union of Marine Aviation and Shipping Transport Officers
> NUMAST is constantly campaigning for increased safety in all areas all the time. It is only by continual lobbying that we can even stand still and repel those who would reduce standards. Often we achieve successes.   (Nov 1995)

Sea Safety Group of Ship Owners Pilots and Captains
> The ferry maze is a danger to passengers. The number of amusement arcades, shops, bars and discos on vessels is growing alarmingly with not enough emergency exit signs. They are small in number and badly placed. Facilities had been maximised to boost profits. Mazes are being created which confused even professional seafarers. Campaigners want evacuation procedures and staff training to be improved. (August 1995)

Chief Officer Jeremy Beech, Kent Fire Brigade.

There will always be a risk of fire at sea and modern ships are better equipped to deal with it. Despite modern techniques to protect engine rooms, we have had to transport our fire fighters by helicopter to be lowered on board, because the ship's fire fighting equipment failed to contain a fire. (1995)

UK ferry captain

The timber panelling on the bridge started to smoulder whilst we were on voyage. I ordered the Chief Engineer to start the main fire pump. He rang back immediately to notify me that the starting handle for the main pump was missing. I then ordered him to start the emergency fire pump, which he did. I left the bridge, lifted a fire hose and attempted to connect it to the fire hydrant when one of the couplings on the hose broke off. I then connected a different fire hose to the hydrant and turned on the water. Within a few seconds the small fire was extinguished. Just as I was about to turn the water off at the fire hose control, the water actually stopped. After clearing away the fire hose, I spoke to the chief engineer and told him never to turn off the fire pump until I ordered him to do so. He replied, I did not turn off the fire pump, we actually ran out of petrol. (April 1996)

Marine Safety Agency

Ship to shore communications should be reviewed to ensure that they provide the quickest possible contact with the fire brigade at all times. Liaison should not be confined to communication matters but should include training and fire-fighting. (1995)

SURVEY OF
SHIPPING OPERATORS

Having taken statements and advice from numerous individuals and organisations among the sea-faring community, researching this book has uncovered a number of important concerns for the safety of those who travel by ship and who will do so in the future.

Fire is a basic element. The incidence of the accidental start of fire will never be totally eradicated on board ships or elsewhere. But experience has shown that sensible and straightforward fire prevention measures work. They prevent the physical disruption caused by fire as well as the emotional upset to those caught up in fire. Sensible and simple fire prevention methods also save lives.

We asked a number of British shipping companies if they would answer some basic questions about fire on their vessels and the measures they take to minimise and deal with its outbreak. As various sections of this book have argued, one basic essential in a fire is the level of training that staff have had, to enable them to deal effectively with the situation.

We asked about the practice of fire drills – tiresome though they can be, they do give vital experience and confidence in dealing with the real thing. And since we recommend strongly that a named individual be responsible in any company for overseeing safety matters we asked these leading British ferry and shipping companies if they have such a system of accountability.

The simple questionnaire had only seven questions as follows. The replies are for the reader to judge on the following pages.

1 How many members of the crew on each vessel has attended a fire fighting course?
2 How many members of the crew on each vessel are qualified to wear breathing apparatus?
3 How regular are fire drills held on board? eg weekly, monthly.
4 Are the fire drills held when passengers are on board?
5 How regular are evacuation drills held?
6 Are the evacuation drills held when passengers are on board?
7 Who is responsible for the regular inspection of the fire fighting equipment and breathing apparatus? eg Chief Officer, Chief Engineer.

V. Ships/Airtours

Air Tours, the well-known holiday company, have two ships which are managed by V Ships.

1 All certified officers attend firefighting courses as part of their training.

Most recruiting agencies we use have a requirement that crew attend a 2 day firefighting course at approx. 5 year intervals.
A company-specific firefighting course is being run – approximately twice a year for senior officers.

2 Varies according to nationalities on board but as an approximate minimum:
80% Deck Officers + crew
60% Engine Officers + crew

3 Weekly fire drills for all crew.
Additional training on a daily basis for specific emergency groups.

4 Yes.

5 Whenever new passengers embark a muster is held.
Stairways guides and passenger muster personnel are given regular additional training.
Ship's company evacuate the ship at least once every 3 months but normally once a month depending on the itinerary.

6 Yes.

7 Depends upon vessel manning, but either Safety Officer (if carried) or if not Staff Captain (who then becomes the Ship's Safety Offficer).

Richard Evenhand
Safety and Maritime Superintendent

SeaCat

> *SeaCat run a ferry service between Belfast and Stranraer with a fast journey time of 90 minutes. They also offer exclusive fares to France and other European destinations using their sister company, Hoverspeed.*

1 SeaCat has three crews: half of these have a Merchant Navy Training Board approved firefighting certificate. These are the crew members designated as firefighters in the event of an accident. All other crew members are trained in-house. This course includes evacuation procedures, first aid and firefighting. A written examination with a 90% pass mark must be achieved before the crew are allowed to go into service.

In addition a three-day emergency response course had been developed with the Fire Service College at Moreton-in-the-Marsh, Gloucestershire. This intensive course is attended by all crew from the most senior, (ie captain) to the most junior as one unit. This ensures a team approach.

2 All those crew members with a Merchant Navy training board certificate and all those who have attended the Moreton-in-the-Marsh course are qualified to wear breathing apparatus. This is in excess of the requirements of the vessel's emergency response team. 49 out of a total of 77 crew members.

3 Fire drills are held on board the craft for each different crew on at least a weekly basis. This involves a different scenario being set on as many occasions as possible with any crew suggestions incorporated. A record is also kept of individual attendance to ensure periods of sickness or

holiday do not interrupt the training schedule.
4 Occasional fire drills are held when passengers are on board.
5 Evacuation drills are held on a weekly basis. See 3 for further details. The emergency drills are witnessed and approved by the Flag Administration and at regular intervals by the Marine Safety Agency.
6 SeaCat Scotland in its commitment to ensure the highest possible safety standards is working towards the future voluntary involvement of passengers.
7 Inspection of ALL safety items is incorporated in a computerised planned maintenance system for which the chief officer is responsible. Updated copies of the planned maintenance schedule are transferred to the technical department ashore, who in turn monitor the performance of the equipment.

The divisions' safety manager, who reports directly to the Vice President of Ferries and Ports at Sea Containers, SeaCat Scotland's parent company, is responsible for monitoring and spot checking safety procedures and equipment in accordance with the company's International Safety Management Code.

Hamish Ross
Managing Director

The Isle of Man Steam Packet Company
Runs regular sailings to Douglas from Heysham,
Liverpool, Fleetwood, Belfast and Dublin

1 All officers have attended a firefighting course at
   approved fire stations.

2 All officers have been trained and all permanent deck
   and engine room ratings have attended a
   breathing apparatus course.

3 General emergency drills are held weekly and a fire
   drill is held in conjunction with this at least twice
   a month.

4 Generally the drills are held in port when there are no
   passengers on board. However, from time to time
   exercises are conducted with the Coastguard and
   rescue services when volunteer passengers are
   involved.

5 Abandon ship drills are held weekly.

6 Same as 4.

7 Chief Officer in all areas outside of machinery spaces.
   Chief Engineer in machinery spaces.

David Dixon
Managing Director

SALLY Vessel Management
Sally line offer a choice of sailings between Ramsgate, Dunkirk and Ostend.

Statement on Safety Policy

Sally Line considers safety as an essential ingredient in its business activities. It holds equal status with other business activities.

Sally Line are committed to provide adequate resources so as to ensure that these objectives are achieved. Our crew are trained to the highest possible standard. Standards that exceed the minimum IMO (Standards on Training Certification & Watchkeeping Convention) requirements.

Training is an ongoing process and joint exercises are arranged with the local Fire Brigade and other emergency services to our mutual benefit.

The safety of our vessels, passengers and crew is considered paramount.

1 All deck and engine crew, chief pursers and cooks have attended a firefighting course. Senior ships staff have also completed an advanced course in Command and Control. (30 per vessel)
2 All fire parties are qualified to wear breathing apparatus. (10 per vessel)
3 Fire drills are conducted weekly.
4 Fire drills are conducted when passengers are onboard and an announcement is made.
5 Evacuation drills are held weekly.
6 Evacuation drills are held when passengers are onboard and an announcement is made.
7 The Deputy Master is responsible for the regular inspection of safety equipment.

Chris Bravery, Marine Safety Manager

Caledonian MacBrayne

> *CalMac run daily ferries on the River Clyde and to*
> *23 Scottish islands. The fleet comprises 30 vessels which*
> *operate from some 52 ports and terminals.*

Our modern fleet of car ferries is fitted with every worthwhile safety device and a fail-safe system of visual, oral reporting and electronic checks are completed on every occasion before a vessel proceeds to sea.

1 Most deck and engineering officers plus most of the deck crew members have attended a Strathclyde Fire Brigade firefighting course which has been specifically devised with this company's requirements in mind.

2 All personnel who have attended the above course are trained in the use of breathing apparatus and, during the course, have to fight a very real fire with dense smoke conditions while wearing breathing apparatus. No formal qualification is given with regard to breathing apparatus.

3 Fire and Abandon Ship drills are held weekly.

4 Fire drills are occasionally held while passengers are on board, although we tend to find that even although passengers have been forewarned of the exercise, they can sometimes feel uneasy seeing crew members moving about wearing lifejackets or breathing apparatus.

5 All fire drills are designed so that 'the fire' eventually gets out of control, leading to a full Abandon Ship exercise.

6 Same as for fire drills.

7 The Chief Officer is responsible for the regular inspection of all firefighting apparatus. At every fire drill, over and above the use of breathing

apparatus, fire hoses, drencher systems, etc, one fire extinguisher is discharged and then refilled at the end of the drill.

To add to the safety of our vessels we have recently fitted, or are in the process of fitting to all our major vessels, a stability loading computer which gives a full and detailed printout of the vessel's stability condition before proceeding to sea.

Captain A B Ferguson
Marine Superintendent

Stena Line

Stena Line offer sailings between Stranraer/Belfast, Holyhead/Dun Laoghaire, Fishguard/Rosslare, Southampton/Cherbourg, Newhaven/Dieppe, Dover/ Calais, Harwich/Hook of Holland. Stena also run an extensive range of sailings between Sweden, Germany, Denmark and Norway.

1 In general all of the deck and engine crew on our vessels have attended Merchant Navy Training Board fire courses of Stage 1, 2 and 3 as appropriate. Passenger service crew have on board training in fire awareness and the use of fire extinguishers, etc.

On all of our fast ferries all crew are 'type-rated' which includes the use of all on board safety equipment. Without exception we have a good working relationship with the Fire Brigade and Coastguard in all our port locations. Consequently we engage in combined fire drills on a regular basis – this includes landing firemen on board by helicopter.

2 In general all of the deck and engine crew will have had SCBA (Self Contained Breathing Apparatus) training. Depending on ship size this will be between 25 and 40 persons on each crew.

3 Fire drills are held weekly on all ships. Stena Line has also developed a shut down procedure for each ship to minimise the effect of engine room and galley fires. These drills are practised monthly.

4 Sometimes fire drills are held when passengers are on board.

5 General emergency and abandon ship drills are held weekly on all ships. They are sometimes held with passengers on board. Recently we have done major evacuation exercises with the Coastguard at

Fishguard, Newhaven and Dover. At Dover we evacuated 723 passengers and 119 crew from the *Stena Invicta*.

6 In general the Chief Engineer looks after the firefighting equipment in the engine room and the Chief Officer looks after the equipment throughout the rest of the ship.

Captain NR Pyke
Head of Safety

P&O European Ferries
> *P & O offer routes to France, Spain and Northern Ireland and the Northern Isles.*

I am in receipt of your letter dated 28 February. The safety of our passengers and employees is of paramount importance to P&O European Ferries and is never compromised. All of our ships comply fully with current national and international rules and regulations relating to crew training and maintenance of life saving appliances. The Training of our Masters, Officers and Ratings is invariably well in excess of statutory requirements.

RD Peters
Managing Director

Color Line

MS Color Viking departs from Newcastle twice a week for Stavanger, Haugesund and Bergen.

1 Fire Fighting Courses

All catering staff on board with less than 3 years sea service have had a contingency course consisting of firefighting, first aid, rescue and ship's knowledge.

All deck and engine crew with less than 3 years service have been on approved safety and security courses – these include extensive firefighting training and all are qualified to wear breathing apparatus. As of today we have 110 crew members who are part of the Alarm Instructions. Of these 101 have been on firefighting courses, the remaining 9 being exempt due to long sea service (92% have therefore attended firefighting courses).

2 Qualified to Wear Breathing Apparatus

All deck and engine crew are qualified to wear breathing apparatus. In addition, most of our chefs are also qualified. All crew who have been on an approved safety course (Leiro I & III) are also qualified. Several of our catering staff are also qualified although this is not a requirement.

MV Color Viking has in its Alarm Instructions 5 firefighting teams with 3 in each team who are qualified to wear breathing apparatus. These have all, in addition to approved firefighting courses, been on a 5-day firefighting course with the Bergen fire brigade, also training in the use of breathing apparatus. These are all sent on an annual refresher course with the Bergen fire brigade.

Of the 110 crew who are part of our alarm

151

instruction, 25 are qualified to wear breathing apparatus (23%). Exercises using smoke are held on board 2-3 times a month.

3 Fire and Lifeboat Drills

These are held 2-3 times a month. In accordance with Norwegian Maritime Laws and Regulations, fire and lifeboat drills are to be held for passengers who are in open sea for more than 24 hours. *Color Viking* is never at sea for more than 24 hours and we therefore do not have any drills directly involving our passengers. Alarm instructions are of course posted in all cabins and safety and security announcements are made in both English and Norwegian upon departure. The chief security officer also holds a safety and security meeting for all passengers on departure.

Fire and lifeboat drills are held whilst the ship is in port and usually there are round-trip passengers on board. Information regarding the various exercises is therefore communicated to the passengers over the loudspeaker system.

4 Inspection of Firefighting Equipment and Breathing Apparatus

Color Line sets safety and security as its main priority and therefore have on all our ships a chief security officer who is, amongst other things, responsible for all safety equipment, including firefighting equipment and breathing apparatus and that these are always kept in full working order.

D Romslo
Manager (UK)

North Sea Ferries

Run daily sailings from Hull to Rotterdam and Zeebrugge.

Please be advised that safety standards on board our ferries meet and exceed both UK and International requirements and indeed as a Company we have already obtained our Document of Compliance under the ISM Code. Also we can confirm that the number of crew members holding various firefighting certificate qualifications is well in excess of the minimum number required by UK regulations.

MA Ranson
Safety and Environmental Superintendent

GLOSSARY

bow	the front of the ship
stern	the rear of the ship
port	left hand side of ship when facing the bow
starboard	right hand side of ship when facing the bow
forward	from the centre of the ship to the bow
aft	from the centre of the ship to the stern
deck no.	eg deck 4 – this would be the equivalent to the 4th floor in a building
bridge	where the navigation, communication and day-to-day running of the ship is controlled by the captain and senior officers
VHF radio	very high frequency radio – range limited to between 30 and 50 miles depending on weather conditions
DFDS	Scandinavian shipping company with a large fleet of ships and a number of subsidiary companies. The *Tor Scandinavia* is managed by one of these companies, Scandinavian Seaways
Ro-Ro	Roll-on-Roll-off vehicle-carrying ship
Class I ship	large ocean going liners and cruise ships
Class II ship	ships on short international voyages and some coastal waters – usually ferries
MAIB	Marine Accident Investigation Branch
IMO	International Maritime Organisation
MSA	Marine Safety Agency

While sailing one day on a cruise to a little island off the east coast of Scotland, a member of the crew stuck his head out of the small cabin, looked the six passengers individually in the eye and made the following safety announcement:

"If anything happens, he'll tell me whit tae dae, (pointing to the skipper) an I'll tell youse."

On sailing to the Isle of Eriskay, made famous by the film *Whisky Galore* the following safety announcement was heard over the tannoy,

"If you should find yourselves over the side, hold on."

Bon voyage!
John & Noreen